CH00802134

Feeding People

For Sarah, Otis and Isis

"Our children are our elders in universe time."

Buckminster Fuller

Feeding People

First published in 2010 by Ecademy Press
48 St Vincent Drive, St Albans, Herts, AL1 5SJ

info@ecademy-press.com
www.ecademy-press.com

Printed and Bound by Lightning Source in the UK and USA

Set in Warnock Pro by Emma Lewis

Printed on acid-free paper from managed forests.

This book is printed on demand, so no copies will be remaindered or pulped.

ISBN 978-1-905823-86-4

The right of Leon Aarts to be identified as the author of this work has been asserted in accordance with sections 77 and 78 of the Copyright Designs and Patents Act 1988.

A CIP catalogue record for this book is available from the British Library.

All rights reserved. No part of this work may be reproduced in any material form (including photocopying or storing in any medium by electronic means and whether or not transiently or incidentally to some other use of this publication) without the written permission of the copyright holder except in accordance with the provisions of the Copyright, Designs and Patents Act 1988. Applications for the Copyright holder's written permission to reproduce any part of this publication should be addressed to the publishers.

Copyright © 2010 Leon Aarts

Contents

Contents

Introduction

Feeding people? What does that mean? Feeding means
so much more than food. We can feed our minds and our
bodies. Which one is more important and which one do
we need to feed first? Can we feed one and not the other?

Millions of people go to bed hungry every night and that is
something I am dedicated to stop. Millions of other people
do have enough to eat but are lonely and feel disconnected. Mother Teresa calls it poverty of the heart. Is it that we
are not connected? What happened to us to get into this
state on our planet?

We are all interconnected and as soon as we truly realise
that and we start to connect with ourselves and connect
with everybody else living on this planet, we can overcome
the challenges we face on this planet. See the end of poverty and restoration of the planet in our lifetime. Everything
you need is already in your heart.

We have the resources within us so that nobody goes to
bed hungry and so that we can all connect with each other
and make this world a better place. When we all find our
purpose and act upon it.

I'll show you through the experiences and learnings of my
own life how you can become the person you really are
by connecting your passion and purpose, living a life you
enjoy and to your fullest potential.

Food has always been an important part of my life. I have

spent many years as a chef and later as a distributor of fine foods. My mother was a great cook and food was also very important in my dad's family. It was the way they communicated. I always seemed to be hungry and the first question I asked all the time was, "What's for dinner?" Still I became a chef by accident. So food is obvious but feeding people means so much more. The rest of my life's journey comes from the lessons I have learned through the challenges and experiences which came on my path. Feeding is a lot more than just food; we need to feed our body and mind and that is what I do. I feed people. In this book I take you on my journey, my story of the alchemist. What happens when you discover your purpose and see that it has been with you all your life?

Business plays a big part in the changes we need to establish on the planet. I have been an entrepreneur all my life and I believe entrepreneurs change the world, governments don't, so a big part of the book is about how you can add your purpose to your business. Use your business to create good and have fun doing it.

We need to become connected again to ourselves and the people around us. Are you looking for change and inspiration to make a difference? I show you how I have done it. I show you that we all can do that. If I can, anyone can; I show you that it is not difficult and that it is in all of us.

My professional life and all my learnings made me realise that everything I need is in me and I have been prepared to follow my purpose. My dream is that we all do that. There is nothing more powerful and wonderful than to live a life of purpose.

Look inside and find your treasure. If I can do it, so can you. I have a vision that nobody goes to bed hungry – not hungry for food or hungry for love or being connected.

Enjoy reading.

Introduction

Chapter 1

It is all in you

Just this week as I am writing this book, a very good friend of me reminded me, she said, "How come we can send people to the moon, we have the technology, and we cannot solve world hunger or poverty? It doesn't make sense." We have the solutions and these wonderful technologies within us, surely we must be able to achieve together the end of world hunger and poverty. Is it that we are not bold enough? Are there other things that are holding us back? In 1960, J F Kennedy said, "Within 10 years, people will be walking on the moon." He had no idea how they were going to achieve it, but he and his team were convinced they were going to do it. And they did! Microsoft started in the seventies and their vision was a computer on every desk. They had no idea how they were going to do it. And they did! So if enough of us really want to make this world a better place, what is holding us back? What do we need to do to truly make this happen?

"We give to live until we live to give."

Michael Beckwith

I believe 100% that everything we achieve in our life is because of us. Also what we don't achieve is 100% up to ourselves. I mean absolutely everything: your successes, your failures, your relationships, your wealth – everything. You have the opportunity to achieve everything you want in life. Again, I mean absolutely everything, it is all in you.

You choose the route you take and the standards you set for yourself. It is not our circumstances which shape us, what shapes us is how we decide to react to them.

Looking inside

We have to look inside ourselves at who we truly are, why we are here and what our purpose and goals are. The answers are all there. Every time I have a challenge I always look inside myself. Why is this showing up in my life, why are the results I was hoping for not showing up? Look inside yourself and the answer will reveal itself to you. This is not easy to start with; it is a process you will have to master and you get better at it over time. I promise you will end up really enjoying it as it is very rewarding. What you are really doing is truly connecting with yourself. Go inside and explore.

Often in life when we face a challenge and we feel we are hitting a brick wall, we often express this feeling. We get frustrated because we don't know a way out. When I come across these situations with others, I often tell them the story about a fly going around in circles in front of a window. The fly sees the other side and wants to go there but doesn't know how to get there. It starts searching frantically for the way out by flying faster, going over the same space all the time. When you see this happening, you open the window next to the one where the fly is flying and, more often than not, the fly doesn't see the open window and keeps flying around until it kills itself. The only thing it had to do is go backwards a bit, maybe 50cm or so, have a look at the situation and it would soon see the open window. Our challenges are exactly the same. Go back for yourself, take a distance and go inside yourself, listen to what is really going on and what you can do about it.

"I wanted to change the world. But I have found that the only thing I can be sure of changing is oneself."

Aldous Huxley

We cannot truly connect to others if we haven't truly connected to ourselves. Some people call it connecting, other people call it love. They say you cannot love others until you love yourself and both are right. Light is the most basic form of energy and for me light is love.

My mother always used to say, "Love is the only thing you can keep giving away without ever running out of it." How right she was. It is always there and in abundance, so why are we holding on to it all the time? Is it something inside ourselves, is it that we don't love ourselves enough or maybe we don't trust ourselves? Why are we holding on to it, and why are we not handing it out all the time?

The answer is inside us. When we explore and really get to know ourselves, we can, and we will, share our love with others. This is the hardest lesson of all, but when you master it a whole new life will open up for you.

"The biggest and hardest lesson I have learned in life is that the external world is just a reflection of the world within."

Tony Hsieh

Many people are looking for answers in their life and don't realise that the answers are always right in front of them. People in general don't like to hear, "It's easy." A difficult solution for some reason sounds more plausible. Well, let me tell you life is not meant to be difficult, the universe is there to help you. Listen to what comes to you and go with it. It really is as simple as that.

Your thoughts are actual things in the universe. Be yourself and you'll see the solutions you need. I always go from the premise that when it is not easy, go back and try again as it is not meant to be hard or complicated. Will Smith, the famous actor, talks about this. When you make a conscious choice for whatever it is in life, go with it and stick with it. If you make a choice, then everything you do, every action, has to support the plan. Too often, when we don't get the results we want we go to Plan B. Will tells you to stick with Plan A whatever the results, because the results you are getting are telling you something and you can change that, but don't change the plan. When you find your purpose, the reason why you are here, how can you ever change your purpose?

Do you think Mahatma Ghandi ever thought to change his plans when he didn't immediately get the results he wanted? He created a huge following without ever having an official role. Did he change his plans when he was on hunger strike and possibly could die very soon? He had a big mission for the people of India and he stuck with that, whatever the challenges were that he came across along the way. Do you think he hoped people would stop fighting just so he was able to eat or do you believe his cause of peace and non-violence was bigger than him? Now, more than 60 years after his death, Ghandi is still one of the most important people in India's history and he will be in hundreds of years to come. His purpose was bigger than him.

A little while ago I saw a great story on ted.com. This great website has hundreds of inspiring talks by leaders in their field. Bertrand Piccard talks about his experience in a hot-air balloon flying around the world non-stop and how that experience taught him about life, himself and growing to another level. One of their experiences was that in order to survive, they had to get rid of all the ballast they had on board, even the extra fuel they had taken. It was the only option they had to gain enough height. A major challenge such as giving up your spare fuel flying in a balloon around the world at 50,000 feet is not something you do easily. Something which went against their instincts and everything they had learnt. He and his co-pilot had to take a huge leap of faith.

Bernard realised later that in this was a very valuable lesson for him. In order to grow in life and to go to a higher level, we have to get rid of all our inner ballast. When we do that we not only go to a higher level, we also go faster. What you need is total trust and faith in yourself, the universe and the people around you. By going to a different level/altitude, you not only gain height, you also have a different perspective on the challenges you face. Gaining altitude means that the atmosphere gets thinner, which makes you move faster.

What is your inner ballast, what is holding you back? Spend some time to really get to know yourself, what makes you tick and the patterns you have occurring in your life? See which changes you want to make in your life. What do you want to achieve? Which ballast do you need to get rid of in order to go to a higher level? A few years ago, when our son Otis was eight, he came to me and said, "I wasn't good at playing football and my friends didn't like playing football with me, but now I have practised and I am a lot better at it. We now play together." This took me back straight away to the moment when I was eight years old. I had a similar experience, I took my challenge totally differently and it shaped me for the rest of my life. I was so proud of Otis taking his challenge in his stride, practising and is now a lot better at football. He wasn't a good player but now he is a goalkeeper in our local club. What he took from a similar experience is that he can be good at anything as long as he enjoys it and as long as he puts his mind to it. I still thank him for that lesson and am so happy he understood very quickly at a very young age.

Discovering your purpose

I often get the following question, "Leon, I would love to make some changes and do some personal development. Which program should I follow?" Often people have read a book or done a program at work or have already spent thousands of pounds on themselves and not really achieved any changes. The answer I give is always the same: "Go to India or Africa for two weeks and spend some time with people who don't have as much as we have, listen and learn from them. Live with them and talk to them. Often these people have an inner peace and are still connected with each other. We can learn so much from them. I guarantee you come back from that trip as a changed person and then do that personal development program you really want to do. I promise you it will be really successful."

In January 2008, we went with the children and about 50 other people from XL to India on a trip with The Hunger Project. It was called the Pioneer Club. XL is a club of social entrepreneurs whose goal is to create World Wide Wealth collectively. XL was set up by Roger Hamilton to empower entrepreneurs, achieving the UN's Millennium Development Goals. The Pioneer Club was some of us members spending time to see how we could make a bigger difference together. We supported the work of The Hunger Project and in the last week of our trip we spent time with The Hunger Project leaders. We learned how they train and teach women leaders in villages in India. The work The Hunger Project does is truly amazing. They empower women to help their whole community to come out of poverty. Seeing their vision workshops in some really rural areas was life-changing. We spoke to women who were illiterate, who had never been spoken to by their own name but were now the local councillor for their village. Their huts were often made of mud and would disappear completely during the first rains. The challenges they had to endure to overcome their poverty were so enormous that I realised when I arrived home from this trip I would never think any more that I had challenges I could not overcome. We spoke to one lady who had to go to a regional office (a four-hour round bus trip) more than 30 times just to ask for more food supplies. Another lady we met decided that, after two years of sending requests to the local government and not getting any replies to her requests to build a water well, they would build one themselves. We saw the result of their work and, after six months of work by 30 women, they still had a few metres and three months to go before they would find water. All done by hand. In India, poverty is not helped by the bureaucracy and caste system.

This trip really touched each one of us; even the children came back different. Standing in a field after The Hunger Project, sharing with us their challenges about fundraising, I realised there must be a better way. Since then, January 2008, I made it my goal to help organisations like The Hunger Project to find better ways of raising funds.

"I see the kids in the street. With not enough to eat. Who am I to be blind pretending not to see their needs?"

Man in the Mirror - Michael Jackson

In order to make real changes in our life we have to find out what our real passion and purpose are. Too many people do things in life which they are not passionate about, go to their job every day hating it but feel they have no choice. I am fortunate enough; I have always done what I am passionate about and, if that wasn't the case, I always stopped, left, and the next thing would come along almost immediately. Never, ever let something you are not happy about hold a space in your life. It blocks the flow of a good thing coming to you on your path. When you cut out or stop whatever it is which blocks you, something you enjoy and feel passionate about will be there immediately. The better you understand what you are passionate about, what you enjoy, the better choices you can make and the quicker your life will move in the direction you want it to go.

So what are you passionate about? The next thing we need to find is our purpose. What makes you come to life, gets you to jump out of bed in the morning? These are the two key things you have to find out about yourself. When you know your passion and have found your purpose and connect these two together, you can make something so powerful it is unbelievable. Your purpose is the reason you are here on this planet.

What is your purpose? In our heart we all know what our purpose is. Allow yourself to go down that path and you'll find your world will change. In the book *The Alchemist* by Paolo Coelho, there is a passage where he says that we all know what our purpose is and what our role is in this life. We all have a big purpose. As a child, you know, but then life steps in and it seems to disappear. It never really does, it is always there, you have just side-stepped it for whatever reason fits you. Teachers, parents or friends tell you that you can't do certain things because you wear glasses; you are too tall; you are not smart enough; or we want you to become a doctor. I am sure you have heard them all. Later in life, for all of us there is a situation where your purpose comes back to you and you have the opportunity to follow it. Most people by then are so stuck, or they believe so, they choose to stay with the life they are living at the time. They have a mortgage, are running a company or maybe they think their team at work can't do without them. Or are you simply afraid of the unknown? The universe always provides you with what you need if you go after your dreams, especially if you have connected and locked your passion and purpose together.

"We must be willing to get rid of the life we've planned, so as to have the life that is waiting for us."

Joseph Campbell

I remember clearly a situation in my youth when I knew what my big purpose was. It was 1973 and I was seven years old; the Ethiopian famine was on television. In those days, Africa was so far removed that we thought we would never go there. It seemed like a different world. We were having family dinner and I didn't want to eat some kind of vegetables. My mother told me to finish my dinner and she said, "There are people starving on the other side of the world who would love to eat those vegetables." It didn't make sense to me as a child how eating those vegetables would help starving children. My thoughts at the time were, 'One day I will do something to help hungry people; at the moment I don't want to eat these vegetables.' I remember that moment really well and it came back to me many years later when I was setting up Extraordinary Ones. Reading *The Alchemist* I knew immediately I had connected my deepest passion and purpose: food, and nobody to bed hungry. When you have that feeling, there is no way, no reason you will ever stop achieving that purpose. My big vision: nobody to bed hungry.

In his famous inauguration speech, Nelson Mandela spoke the famous quote by *Marianne Williamson: "Our deepest fear is not that we are inadequate. Our deepest fear is that we are powerful beyond measure. It is our light not our darkness that most frightens us. We ask ourselves 'Who am I to be brilliant, gorgeous, talented and fabulous?' Actually, who are you not to be? You are a child of god. Your playing small does not serve the world. There is nothing enlightened about shrinking so that other people won't feel insecure around you. It is not just in some of us; it is in everyone. And as we let our own light shine, we unconsciously give other people permission to do the same."*

As Marianne says, it is in all of us and we don't serve anyone by playing it small and not being that person we should be. Light is the most basic form of energy. So being the light means being truly you and by being yourself you help and inspire others. You shine at your brightest when you are truly 100% yourself. A candle can light thousands of other candles. What that means is that it doesn't cost you any energy by being 100% yourself to inspire others. When you go out of your way, not being totally yourself, you lose your energy really quickly. It costs a lot more energy trying to play it down just because others might feel insecure around you. Changing yourself just to comfort others costs you energy and doesn't serve anyone. Others who don't see the world in the same way you do are still playing at a different level; they basically still need to lose a bit more ballast.

Challenges

You can see Deepak Chopra in a great video called *The Wonder of You*. In this one-minute video he talks about when you are born you have 100 trillion cells in your body. Each cell instantly knows what the other cells do and what their role is. How does a human body organise its thoughts, play a piano, clean toxins, make a baby all at the same time, while following the rhythm of the cosmos? This is because we have an inner intelligence called our consciousness and our consciousness mirrors the cosmos.

When you are born, everything functions immediately, every cell knows what to do and how to interact. A cell in your toes can communicate with a cell in your brain. Our inner intelligence can tap into the wisdom of the universe and we consist of over 100 trillion cells which all interact with each other and know what to do. If we believe that all our cells are connected to each other and collectively are connected to everything which happens around us, what would happen if we accept that?

Accept that everything is already all right as it is; everything we need is already there for us. We can tap into it now. That is such a powerful realisation. Everything you need is already in you.

Nature has a rhythm and so has life. The rhythm of the universe is its heartbeat, it keeps everything moving forward. When we accept the rhythm of life it is much easier to move, find our true purpose and go to the next level. Too many people worry about things they cannot influence. In nature, for example, autumn comes after summer – it has been doing so for millions of years and it will do for millions of years to come. And so will rain, storm, hot or cold weather come and go. Everything has its place in nature. When we start to see pattern in our own life we can then accept the pace of life. Accept what comes your way, work with it, follow the seasons in your life, don't fight it and understand why you have certain patterns in your life.

To give you an example: in London, the winter of 2010 was one of the coldest winters the UK had experienced for about 30 years. Snow stopped the city a few times which is very rare. Many businesses were up in arms, worrying that they couldn't reach their customers with their deliveries and worried about loss of turnover because of the snow. You can't change the weather so accept it and work with it. Find solutions, talk to your customers and you find by relaxing, working with the challenge, everything solves itself. Use the snow as an extra opportunity to talk to your customers and improve your relationship with them. I saw too many people focusing on what they couldn't do.

When you see the patterns, go into yourself and find what you need to do in order to make improvements. Like the title of this chapter says: it is all in you.

If you live a life in flow, enjoying every moment, doing the things you love, fulfilling your purpose, you can handle every situation which comes your way with much more ease. You understand why certain situations come on your path and how you need to deal with them. Life will have a different meaning. You choose the level you want to play at and be happy with.

Mother Teresa definitely lived a life of purpose. She chose to help other people and everything she needed showed up for her. She was so confident that God provided for her that every Sunday evening she gave away all the spare money they had, trusting that the universe would provide them with everything they needed. It always did and never failed. By the time of her death, her organisation was running over 400 homes for children and poor or sick people.

In August 2007 I was in Bali for the second time for a program called EBS Masters. To me it was the best and most life-changing program I have ever done. As a winner of the previous EBS, I was offered a place: 12 participants, seven mentors, one week. One of the most profound insights that week was one night over dinner when I realised that we are all born with certain challenges in our life. We can do two things: accept them and work with them or try to fight them all our life. This sounds very simple and really it is. With everything else happening that week, I realised that I had been trying to fight some of my challenges all my life. What would change if I just accepted them and used them to my advantage?

This proved to be a test of character. On the plane home from EBS masters I decided that, from now on, I would only live a life of purpose and enjoy life. When life is a game and we have all the tools to play the game, to face our challenges, we might as well start to enjoy it. Games are here to have fun.

"Character can't be developed in ease and quiet. Only through experience, trial and suffering can soul be strengthened and success achieved."

Helen Keller

During a presentation in Bali I was asked a few times to explain my background, meaning what I had done before: starting as a chef, restaurateur and selling food. I took this in a totally different way and started to think about who I am, why I am doing what I am doing. What I have learned from my parents and how I have interpreted their experiences on a conscious level. That was very profound; all of a sudden I saw things I had never realised before. I saw the patterns of my own life.

My mum and dad started their own business together
when they were 24 years old – very young but they had
a dream and followed it. Starting a business at the end
of the sixties was different then from how it is nowadays;
there were fewer resources or support available. Both had
a typical working-class background and by working hard
they built up a good business. My parents believed that
by working hard and doing it yourself you could achieve
whatever you wanted. They also thought that there was
no support for business owners, you had to do it all on
your own. Life as an entrepreneur is hard. Unconsciously I
took over these emotions. As an entrepreneur, you need to
work hard, have hardly any support and you have to find it
out all by yourself.

Starting to see those patterns was new to me and very
powerful; realising they were there and recognising them
helps you to change them and you cannot change until
you recognise them. When we started our restaurant
and also our wholesale business, I unconsciously had the
mindset that you could only achieve your dreams through
hard work and doing it on your own and that is how I ap-
proached both businesses. It took me many years and even
more challenges to see that life and business can be a lot
easier.

Sarah and I always thought we had to do it all on our own
– a belief which we both gained from our parents and, as
both of us had that belief, we made it even stronger. For
a long time we weren't aware of the concept of mentors
or anything like that. It wasn't until our wholesale com-

pany really started growing that I realised there are many resources out there to help and support you. As soon as we stopped believing we had to do it all on our own, the business started expanding. We saw that everything we needed was there for us. Support, systems, incubators, mentors –you name it, it was there.

With our beliefs, to prove ourselves, we became some of the best chefs in Holland and later built a great wholesale food business in London in a few years. It made me realise what we could achieve if we focused all that energy in the right way. Use the lessons we learnt and free ourselves from some thoughts which were hampering us. Could we build a business that gives back in a huge way? On a global scale this time, with a great team, enjoying life at the same time in our purpose and passion.

A Matter of Time

A football player practises for hours, rehearsing every move and situation. Yet in a match, they score and win the game on intuition and reflexes. The hours of practising allows them to become masters and build their intuition so they can tap into the rhythm of everything around them. Top players are in flow when they are playing the game and know intuitively what to do. Life is the same if you get in the flow of life. How do you get into flow? That happens when you are totally immersed in an activity you have mastered. You get in the flow of life by removing all obstacles; follow the path of least resistance, find it in yourself.

"People who are focussed on their life mission draw opportunities. Their certainty of who they are and where they are going acts as a drawing card for others to align and assist. People love to be around those who are purposeful."

John Demartini

When you master something, you are totally in your flow; you can actually slow down time. You are a master at the subject; it has become second nature to you so you can react quickly. What happens is that your consciousness goes up and time slows down. An example of this is when you are really enjoying yourself, when you are 'in' the moment. Let's say you are in a meeting for an hour and you are totally present, focused on the person you are with. You achieve a lot more than normally. Consciousness went up so time slowed down. The opposite happens when your consciousness goes down – time will speed up. When you go to sleep you slow down your consciousness and you speed up time. An eight-hour sleep seems to be over in minutes.

When you realise you can do this it is a very powerful attribute to make the most of at any moment. There have been many pieces written about the meaning of time. I am by no means an expert but am very interested in the subject. Time is a phenomenon of the conscious mind. Time has to do with the gravity we experience here on Earth and the speed at which Earth is moving through the universe. Some astronauts have come back with amazing stories about their insights on being in space and what that has done to their beliefs. The best examples are Wubbo Ockels and Edgar Mitchell. There is no such thing as time; only the gravity we experience here on Earth means that we all experience the same time. Wubbo explains that in space where there is no gravity you experience time in a whole different way. Our time is what we experience here on Earth. If we were in a different universe, we would experience time totally differently. We measure our time against the speed of light and, of course, this is always correct as it is our time. Imagine that you are somewhere else and you experience time differently. Would you see a different part of reality? You'd have a different perspective, wouldn't you? So that means there could be much more in the universe but we don't experience it, we can't see it. There could be a whole world out there living in a different perspective from ours and we don't see each other.

Our brain has a program to cope with the speed at which we move through the universe so it feels as if we are not moving at thousands of miles an hour. Imagine you are on one of those children's roundabouts which turn really fast. When you jump off and all of a sudden stop going round, it feels weird because your brain needs a split-second to adjust. This split-second feels longer as you were at a different speed than the ground on which you landed, so time felt slower.

So imagine what there is all around us, what is it we can't see?

If we take ourselves away from that, we can come up with expounding ideas and open ourselves up to whole new ideas of seeing the world and what is around us. Unconsciously, we can tap into everything we need because we are not limited by time. If there is no such thing as time we would always be living in the present. What a gift that would be! Would we see a different world? A world with endless possibilities?

"A master hits a target nobody else can hit, a genius hits a target which no-one else can even see."

Daniel Priestley

A few hundred years ago, natives living on small islands couldn't even imagine the possibility of large boats with more than a hundred people on them travelling the sea. For them this was so impossible that they couldn't even see the ships. The only reason the natives discovered the first boats of people like Columbus was that the chiefs realised the ripples of the sea changed and that there had to be something else going on.

Would you Reset?

Imagine there could be such a thing as the human reset button. Imagine that you could reset your life. You'd have to think about this well as you can only press it once. Press the red button and your life will be reset from where you started; all your lessons, experiences – good and bad – will be gone, you restart afresh. Would you do that or would you leave everything as it is now? Respect your learnings and keep growing? See them all as an important part of you; lose the ballast and move to a higher altitude? What would you do? I am proud and happy with all the learnings I have had in my life and it makes me the person I am now. I look forward to the future, realising that everything I want to achieve is in me and I have the possibilities to do so.

Is there anything you would do differently?

I believe we shouldn't live in the past. Take the lessons
and move on. Live in the now, or in the moment. One of
the best quotes I have ever heard is: *Yesterday is the past,
tomorrow is the future I live today and that is why it is
called 'the present'.* That is exactly what we should be doing
– living in the present.

Chapter 2

You might as well enjoy life!

In the previous chapter I said, 'You might as well enjoy life.' I believe that we live this life to have fun and enjoy it. True, we have our challenges; they are just part of life. It is part of the game; when we enjoy everything we do, our perspective changes and we have a different view on absolutely everything around us.

"Live as if you were to die tomorrow and learn as if you live forever."

Mahatma Gandhi

When we are born, we already have 100 trillion cells in our body – more than there are stars in the universe – and every cell knows what to do. So let's stop trying to figure out what we need to do. Life has a natural rhythm, it is the way nature works and it is the way we are connected, the rhythm of life. Everything has a rhythm or flow; if you tap into your flow you go naturally with what is best for you. You find your path of least resistance. When you tap into your own rhythm, connect with your inner self, the right opportunities will come to you and always at the right time.

Let me give you a few examples of this. In the last year at the hotel college, I had to do two six-month stages in different establishments around the world. We had to finish our education with practical experience. The second stage I did was at the restaurant Paul Bocuse in France, one of the top restaurants in the world at the time. At the end of my stay there they offered me a full-time position three times. It was very rare for a *stagiaire* to be offered a permanent job there. A great opportunity but something inside me told me that I needed to move on. During my time in France, I met managers from Trust House Forte, a huge hotel chain. They offered me a job in the UK which I saw as my stepping-stone to travel the world, working in top restaurants. After I finished in France, I was home for two weeks and left straight away for my first position with them in Oxford. On my first day there I met Sarah, we clicked immediately and she is now my wife. This story is now 20 years old and thankfully I made the right decision. If I had waited and taken the job in France, I might have never met her.

Later, when we had had our restaurant for two years, I realised I had achieved my goal of becoming No.1 at something. The best chefs in Holland at the time told me I was better than they were at the same age. This was 1995 and I didn't realise until many years later that my drive for being a chef had gone. I needed a new goal and it took me another five years to find it. In the summer of 2000, I decided to stop being a chef and look for something different. I didn't know what but I 'knew' intuitively that, before the end of the year, the right opportunity would be there which would take us to the next level. It also would mean doing something totally different, even though at the time I had no idea what it would be. In November I had a call from a friend to explore selling food in London. In the months in between I had a great time; I worked as a consultant, our son was just born, I did a few courses and had lots of time off. We went to London, had a look and, a month later, the first week of January, we moved to London and started our new adventure. We all have stories like this one; when you make the right decision, the speed of events occurring is unbelievable.

Think of the people you know who have fun in their life and enjoy every moment of it. We all know people who do what they enjoy and, because that is what they do, life seems to become even more fun for them. What you appreciate appreciates. It is simply that what you focus on comes your way.

Nick Vujicic was born with no limbs and he lives an extraordinary life, travelling the world motivating youngsters to love life and be happy. He shows them that sometimes you fall down and you feel there is no hope. That doesn't matter; what matters is how you finish and you always find the strength to get back up. He definitely has fallen many times and needed the strength to get back up every time. Have a look on the web and see how emotionally people react and connect with him at the end of his events. He is an incredible role model because if Nick can say, "Hi, my name is Nick Vujicic, I love life and I am happy," we all should be able to do so. Find him on YouTube and be amazed.

I love where he says, "Failing is not not achieving, failing is to stop trying. After you fall the 100th time you get up again the 101st time." One of the best examples we have seen in the last few years confirming that you shouldn't give up is Susan Boyle. Living on her own in a small Scottish village, she was discovered when she was 47 years old; she had been singing since she was 12. She never stopped believing and when she finally had the chance, she grabbed it. Susan's rendition of *I dreamed the dream* is one of the biggest reality show successes we have ever seen and is still being watched by millions.

I have said I believe it is in all of us, we can all achieve our dreams. We don't have to wait 35 years like Susan. Look into yourself, see what is holding you back, tap into the flow and accelerate. When Susan was ready, the right chance presented itself to her – not earlier, at the right time.

We can choose the level at which we want to play the game. Do you want to play Saturday amateur league football or do you want to play on a professional level? Do you think playing any game on a higher level is more fun? You get better by playing with better players and at a higher level you even get paid just to play the game. Spectators pay just to watch a game. Professional football players have a lot of fun, they do what they love, get paid and by playing often they have even more fun, maybe even playing for their national team. A good example of somebody who is at the top of his game and everybody knows is Simon Cowell. Simon realised where he could make a difference, what he can do better than others and started to play that game. Now he is very successful, has lots of fun and by doing that becomes even more successful.

Very often we don't really start to enjoy ourselves until we are a bit older and have had many life lessons. My grand-dad, Bompa, definitely had many challenges in his life. He had to marry very young during the Second World War so he didn't have to go to Germany. He worked in the coal mines during bombings in the war which must have been one of the most terrifying experiences of his life. He also worked two jobs most of his life to provide food for his family with nine children. I like to remember him how he was a few years ago, helping us out when we had our restaurant, doing odd jobs, building our wine cellar and looking after the garden. Every day he asked me to come and pick him up, there was nothing more rewarding than to see him smile. He enjoyed helping his children and grandchildren and seeing them succeed. Later in life he really learned how to love life.

How to enjoy

Paul Hawken, environmentalist and author of the book *Blessed Unrest, How the Largest Movement in the World Came into Being and Why No One Saw It Coming* said in his 2009 opening speech, *"What if the stars would only come out every 100 years, we would all stay up that night."* That is so true. Many of us have got stuck in the life we live, we live in our own bubble and we don't see any more the real beautiful things around us, the things which life is really about.

What if we were to enjoy more what is already around us? Live in the moment and experience everything which is there. Use all your senses and just feel. Come out of your bubble and feel, see, touch, taste and smell what is around you. If you live truly in the moment and you really use all your senses to experience the world around you, there is no space for little voices telling you what you don't have or what isn't perfect in your life. You will enjoy 100% what is there already and you will realise that is a very powerful experience. What have you missed all the time so far and what didn't you see? Only because you were living in your own world and, by doing that, you missed out on so much. There is an easy exercise to practise this. Go for a walk and use all your senses very consciously, experiencing what happens around you. What do you hear, feel and what do you see? You will experience that your walk is totally different from anything you have experienced before and that any thoughts which you had on your mind vanish. There is only one thing to do: enjoy the experience and you will be enjoying it at a whole new level.

Life is really about enjoying many small things. A few weeks ago, our children wanted to walk to school on their own for the first time. That is not a problem except that there is one fairly busy road to cross. We agreed I would walk halfway with them and help them cross the busy road, where I would go back home. When I turned, I kept looking at them secretly and I felt so proud seeing them walking to school, feeling responsible and taking care of each other. Such a small thing, looking at your children, but I still feel proud thinking about that moment. It also made me aware of keeping enjoying the little things more in life and being more appreciative. It is so easy to forget.

We all have a little list of small moments we treasure. We can have those moments all the time – why not try it? What are your small treasures? Is it a dinner with friends or family all having fun around the table, watching your children when they are in bed asleep not aware that you are there? These moments of joy don't have to be just in your private life, they can be in your business or working life as well. Find out what it is for you. Many people believe there is a parallel universe where you experience the same things as you do in your own life, only more pleasurably. My question is always "Why don't you step into that parallel universe now, what holds you back?" I never really get an answer. Because it is the same universe, the same experiences, it is just how you decide to deal with them and which emotions you attach to it.

*"Living consciously involves being genuine, listening and responding to others honestly and openly.
Being in the moment."*

Sidney Poitier

The joy of business

At an event I attended a few years ago, an interviewer asked Sir Richard Branson what in his business would worry him so much it made him stay awake at night. Richard answered, "Nothing." Surprised, the interviewer asked again, "Surely there must be something which keeps you up at night? You run multibillion dollar companies." Now Richard said, "There is nothing in business which keeps me awake at night. It is business, that is all it is, not worth worrying about. Sure, you worry about family when there is something wrong with one of them, but not about business." Wow, that was a powerful lesson which I wished I had heard many years earlier. I have definitely worried in the past about my businesses; when sitting there in Westminster, I promised myself I would never worry about business again.

A good friend of mine, Alan, has been company director to a few very large companies with turnovers of hundreds of millions of dollars. On a trip to Germany to do a presentation for the stock exchange, there he confided to a colleague that he was nervous and had lost a lot of sleep over his presentation and potentially losing a lot of money for the company. The colleague said to him, "Don't worry, it is just a game and that is how you have to look at it." Alan was shocked; to him, lots of money and reputation was at stake, not something to take lightly. The next day, after a great night's sleep, he got up reflecting and he resigned. He now does something totally different – what he loves and enjoys doing.

In order to enjoy life to the fullest, you have to find your passion and purpose. These are in you and you find them by going into yourself and seeing what you enjoy doing and finding out what makes you come alive. What do you want to be known for? If you have problems answering these questions, find a friend or coach or someone you can talk to who can help you in answering these questions. Don't be satisfied until you have really found what that is for you and it resonates with every bone in your body.

A big help to really start to get to know and understand yourself would be to do a profiling test. We are all good at certain things, mostly the ones we enjoy doing, and not good at other things. A good profiling test will help you establish that. The things we are good at are the things which come naturally to us.

There are several different profiling tests out there and you should choose the one with which you feel comfortable. The ones I really like and find the most useful are Innate and the Wealth Dynamics test. Innate is based on colours.

Light is the basic energy; when you break light up you get the colours. This is really interesting as Innate looks at us as being a certain shade of light. Wealth Dynamics is developed on the basis of the I Ching. Both will give you an insight into what you are best at and the areas which are not your strength. Often we are told in life or business that we have to be good at everything. This means we often end up doing jobs we don't enjoy and find hard work. Doing one of these profiles will make you understand why you are good at some things and not at others. Use this as an advantage and focus on the things you are best at. When you do what you are naturally best at you will enjoy it more, get better results and you will become successful. Too many of us spend time on things we are not good at and we don't enjoy. Consequently, we get stressed, frustrated or even ill, only because we are doing things which are taking us out of our natural flow. So remember, in life and business try to do as much as you can of the things you enjoy and which you are naturally best at. It will not only benefit you but definitely the people around you and your relationship with them.

In Wealth Dynamics I am a creator profile which means I am very innovative and intuitive, a 'big picture' thinker and very good at starting things. I am not so good at finishing something, spreadsheets or details. This means that I make my wealth through my ideas. Looking back at my life, that makes a lot of sense and things came naturally when I was making new menus as a chef or starting something totally new like our wholesale business. It also proves that I went out of flow; things became harder when what was required from me was not one of my natural strengths. This happened, for example, when our wholesale business had grown and it was more about running and motivating the team. In the last two years, I have learned how to apply this and use my skills to my advantage and seek help or support from others when what is required is not in my skill set. In building Extraordinary Ones, I have focused on creating the process and getting it off the ground. When building the team, we have kept that in mind and we now have a great team of people, all complementing each other. It helped me enormously to only do what I am best at and what I enjoy and this has had a massive effect on the results we are achieving. People see and feel the joy we are creating within Extraordinary Ones and they want to be part of it.

"Everyone has a mission, everybody has a purpose. It is an expression of their highest values or priorities. Identify what your hierarchy of values is: what is really important to you, the areas of life that are most meaningful to you. Then set goals that are congruent to that and watch how you automatically electrify and energize your life."

John Demartini

A while ago, one of my best friends, Iain, co-founder of Extraordinary Ones who lives in Australia, joked to me when he said, "Leon I am not suggesting you Google all day, drink some coffee and sometimes ring somebody." I started laughing and said, "You are absolutely right, that is all I do every day. It is what I love doing." By creating Extraordinary Ones I also created the best possible job imaginable for myself.

Stephen Covey wrote a great book a few years ago called *The Speed of Trust.* He talks about the speed at which things move when trust is established. We all know this works between friends, family or relations; when there is trust you can accomplish things very quickly, simply getting things done because you trust each other. People and also businesses show up for you and do things for you simply because they trust you. Trust is one of the key things in the relationships between ourselves and others in this life. The question is, how can we trust others if we don't even trust ourselves? Trusting ourselves comes first; if we don't trust ourselves, how can we expect others to trust us?

Enjoyment works in exactly the same way; when you enjoy what you do, that will show to other people. They will see it and react to it. They will connect with you because they can see and feel that you are doing something you love and enjoy, that you are good at it. We should call it the Speed of Joy. It will go ever faster; the more you start to enjoy everything, the more enjoyment you will see. More and more good things will be attracted to you. Opportunities will show up and people will just want to hang out with you. Trust and joy is all within you. Be yourself and allow yourself.

What is your wealth?

This is a question which is debated very often by many people and to which we all put a different meaning. Many of us see wealth mainly as money; how much money we have, the value of our houses, assets, the size of our bank account. Wealth can mean many different things: money, knowledge, connections, assets, family, experience. They are all different energies. For me, the best definition of wealth is: Wealth is everything you have left after you have lost all your money. Money is just one definition and comes and goes in your life. Often that happens unexpectedly, as we have seen, for example, in the recent financial crisis. Your real wealth is the relationships you have, your knowledge and your experience. This wealth nobody can ever take away from you, whatever happens. When you realise this and you have built your knowledge, experiences and relationships, you look at life and its experiences in a whole new light. We need money in our lives to pay for the things we want, our food and our houses. Money, on the other hand, only has the value we put on it and in our modern life we put far too much emphasis on it. Too many people are stuck in jobs they hate because they feel they need a big house or car and feel pressurised by the people around them. You can see them in the traffic jams to work, or lining up waiting for the train. They feel that having more will make them happier. In the western world we live in a 'lie' of ever wanting more to be happier. By believing that we need ever more stuff, we have lost what life is really about and have become too serious. We have lost enjoying what happens around us, enjoying nature, friends and seeing what is really going on.

What could you let go of? What would you need to do in order to just enjoy again?

The time we spent in India in 2008 taught me many things about the joy of life. Poor people, mostly, are not yet trapped by the 'lie' of the West, the idea that we need ever more in order to be happy. It is a very interesting story when you look back in history and see how we have changed. Many years ago, we all lived within our own groups, villages or tribes. We lived off the land. Nature provided us with what we needed and we only took what we needed. There was a balance. As we evolved, we started farming, growing crops and keeping animals. Slowly we wanted more. First we traded some vegetables for milk, grain for a table with a carpenter and later we invented money to make trading easier.

Lynn Twist was one of the early people in The Hunger Project and she also wrote one of my favourite books, *The Soul of Money*, in which she talks about this. Lynn is co-founder of the Pachamama Alliance to help the indigenous Achuar tribe in the Amazon rainforest. If you ever have the chance to see her, please go as she is one of the most inspiring people you will ever meet. Lynn talks about the fact that, at some point in history, we started putting our stakes in the ground and claiming that a certain patch of land was ours. We believed that not only the land was ours but also everything grown on it or found above it or deep in the ground. We started fighting over what we believed was rightly ours. But is it ours? The indigenous tribes of this world still live in harmony with nature, just as we did many years ago when there was a balance. Now we have lost that balance. When we claimed the land as ours, we started using the trees, oil and everything else we found as resources. They are not resources; we started abusing the planet so much that nature can't restore itself any more at the same speed that we are using it. The balance is gone because we believe we have the right to just take. Wars are fought over land and what grows on it. We have lost our connection with each other and with the planet. In the last century, this process has gone ever faster as we found many ways to produce more stuff – bigger, faster, cheaper and more. At the moment, we, the human race, are using three and a half times the resources of what the planet can give us. In the West it is more like seven times, so we are using seven times the amount that Earth can provide. We are out of balance and this needs to be restored.

"We can't have peace on this earth until we have peace with this earth."

Roger Hamilton

In a later chapter I will talk more about this. I believe that together we have all the solutions within us. When we disconnected from each other and started claiming land and what is growing on it to be ours, I believe that is when it started to go wrong. We lost sight of what is really important. That doesn't mean we need to give up everything immediately. The Achuar people say that the world will come together when the condor and the eagle meet. The condor is a metaphor for the indigenous people and the eagle a metaphor for us from the West. When our two cultures come together and work together combining both our learnings, then we will see a turning point on this planet. What it means is that we have to learn from indigenous people how they are connected with each other and with nature, how we used to be, and combine that with our modern day technology. Create a world where we live together and have 'enough', look together at what really counts and what we really need to care more about each other.

What a joy that would be!

Chapter 3

We need to become connected again

I believe that our loss of connection is the root of the problems we are facing today. How come that we can send people to the moon and we can't end world hunger, poverty or the environmental crisis? Is it that we don't have the solutions within us or do we find it easier to work on something which takes us away from real problems and really connecting with each other? Is there something we are scared of, do we not want others to see our true feelings? Are we afraid of being vulnerable?

It is humanity which is missing

It is humanity which is missing. It is the missing link within many things we do. We very often make decisions based on our ego, what we think is best for ourselves. When we turn that around and we look first at how we can serve others, the people around us, we actually realise that we benefit from that ourselves. We see that the greatest gift we can give is ourselves.

When you truly go into your heart and open it up, then you can connect with everyone again. When we see that everything we need is already in us, we will be able to tap into our inner wisdom, our consciousness. This allows us on an energetic level to find the right partner, relationships, lovers and opportunities for us. This will give us the opportunity to connect on a one-to-one level, truly connect from one human being to another.

A good example of how we can connect and, in the process, create huge change is Fateh Singh. In 1998, Fateh established a program in Rathamborne called Tiger Watch. Tiger Watch identified the local Moghiya tribe as one of the major threats to the survival of the local tiger population. For many years, these tribes have been living off the proceeds of tiger poaching, as this was their only means of survival. The wildlife trade gave them money, and the tiger meat provided food. The tiger population in India has been declining very quickly in the last few years and the tiger is in danger of existing only in history books very soon.

But the Moghiyas were keen to give up poaching in favour of alternative means of livelihood. The Tiger Watch program is now teaching the Moghiya tribe more sustainable ways of making a living and, at the same time, educating their children that there is a life away from being a poacher. Through education, the children are being taught about grassroots conservation and how important the tiger is to survival.

Ultimately in India, no tiger means no life. You see, the end of the tiger population has much wider ramifications. In India, many believe the tiger is the protector of the woods; if the tiger disappears, the woods will too. Where there are no woods, there will be no water, and no water means no life. A special hostel has now been set up for the Moghiya boys, where they receive uniforms, clothing, meals and study materials for their education. They also attend school. The Moghiya girls' families are paid a monthly sum for every girl child that the family sends to school. They also receive uniforms and books and their school fees are paid.

The children have become gatekeepers for the protection of the tigers, helping to secure the tigers' future for many generations. Fateh opened his heart and looked how he could create a real solution for one of India's big problems. He connected with the people on the other side of the scale – the poachers – a tribe which wasn't welcomed anywhere, and Fateh decided to work with them.

"The heart of your power is in the power of your heart."

Roger Hamilton

The solution is in your heart. Open your heart. It is the real humanity which is missing within all of us. Earlier I told you that light is the basis of all energies; love or light. When we expand our love to ourselves and each other, our world will open up.

Bus Driver Jorge Munoz has been doing something truly extraordinary. Since 2004 Munoz has served nearly 70,000 free meals and is still going strong! Munoz, who is the founder of An Angel in New York, delivers as many as 140 meals to the hungry people of New York on a nightly basis. If that's not extraordinary enough, he personally funds his operation on his weekly $700 pay cheque!

"I'll help anyone who needs to eat. Just line up," Munoz says. For many, this is their only hot meal of the day; for some, it's the first food they've eaten since last night.

Watching Munoz, aged 44, distribute meals and offer extra cups of coffee, it's clear he's passionate about bringing food to hungry people. For Jorge it is simple; when he sees all these men every night, it is like seeing himself 20 years ago when he first went to America. Jorge connected, looked in his heart and saw what he could do. What Jorge does is truly astonishing.

Women in general care more for the world around them than men. They do that naturally and that is why we have some very successful initiatives which support women to help their communities come out of poverty. One of the most successful initiatives is Grameen Bank from Muhammed Yunus, set up over 30 years ago starting with $27, helping 50 individuals with microloans. Now microfinance is one of the most effective ways of helping people out of poverty. Grameen has given out millions of loans to groups of women as this is the most effective way. Not only will women use the money they make for their immediate family and distribute it, by giving the loans in groups, Grameen ensures that, through peer pressure, the women will focus together on the repayment of the loans. Muhammed Yunus has provided poor people on this planet with a huge service. He saw a problem and realised he could help by lending money to 27 people who had less than him. Out of those first loans, a worldwide movement has grown.

We are part of a bigger picture

Edgar Mitchell was an astronaut on Apollo 14 and the sixth person to walk on the moon. Edgar was travelling back to Earth, having just walked on the moon, when he had a life-transforming experience for which nothing in his life before had prepared him. He saw the Earth rise and realised the stars were like the molecules in his body. He understood immediately that the beautiful blue world to which he was returning is part of a living system, harmonious and whole, and that we all participate, as he expressed it later, 'in a universe of consciousness'. This experience radically altered his worldview. Despite science's superb technological achievements, he realised that we had barely begun to probe the deepest mystery of the universe – the fact of consciousness itself. He became convinced that the uncharted territory of the human mind was the next frontier to explore. He founded the Institute of Noetic Sciences in 1973.

This view might be way out there for some people, but it confirms the general understanding that we are all part of a bigger whole. More and more of us realise each of us is part of something bigger. What if we see each of us as a cell of the universe and each cell as a citizen? We learned earlier that in our body each cell knows what to do, interacts with other cells and they work perfectly together. If we as citizens see each other as cells we need to work with, that we are part of something bigger and one can't progress without the others taking part, when we are connected in that way, we will feel part of the whole universe and tap into its consciousness. Everything we want to achieve will be possible for us.

We would have all access to:

- our collective resources

- our collective wealth

- our collective knowledge

- our collective experiences

- our collective finances

"Death is not the greatest loss in life. The greatest loss is what dies inside us while we live."

Cousins

We have all had the feeling sometimes that something has happened to you and you felt it was meant to be. Or that you meet somebody and you had the idea you have known that person for longer. Other people have been in situations and they felt they have been in that situation before, although they can't explain why or how.

These feelings come from our intuition, also called consciousness. I have learned to always trust my intuition. We are part of a bigger picture and our consciousness reminds us of that. It guides us in the right way in situations if we are open for it.

The power of gratitude

"Gratitude has the potential to change everything from its ordinary state to being a gift."

Unknown

Many books have been written about gratitude. Gratitude: the state of being grateful; thankfulness. Living a life of gratitude and being thankful for everything which comes our way is very powerful. When you become grateful for everything around you, the small things such as the leaves on the trees, birds singing, your family, your house, it will put you in a different mindset – a mindset which allows you to see only the good things and to focus on the good things in life. What you appreciate appreciates. You can practise being grateful, you get better at it over time. And guess what? It doesn't cost you anything, it will actually give you energy; it is one of the most instantly rewarding actions you can take.

By being grateful you will see you have many things in life to be grateful for. You find that your challenges are not always as demanding as you see them. Being grateful also really helps you to deal with the challenges in life and overcome them easily. Dave Rogers is a great coach who lives in Singapore. A few years ago, he was lucky enough to have dinner with Bill Clinton and he could ask him just one question. He asked him, "Mr Clinton, you meet so many unbelievable people, from the general public like me to well-known people; how do you prepare yourself for all these meetings?" Clinton answered, "Before I enter a room, I take a moment for myself and I thank the people for being there and that I am grateful to meet them." That was a really powerful answer and shows partly why Clinton is so successful. People feel on an energetic level the attention and thought you give to them. When you are truly appreciative of them they return that to you even more. This explains a big part of Clinton's success with people.

"Gratitude is not only the greatest of virtues, but the parent of all the others."

Cicero

Gratitude can be expressed in a well-meant 'thank you' when someone has done something for you. It sounds really simple but it makes a big difference – not just in the other person's life, mainly in your own. Simple things such as a bus driver who has waited for you just a bit longer then needed, the shopkeeper going out of his way to help you, the paper boy or a friend coming around when you need it.

It helps you look at other people differently and feel a bit more connected to them again. When you are really thankful to somebody, I assure you they will pass it on to somebody else and it comes back to you.

Connect and create magic

A few years ago my wife and I did a little experiment. A friend of ours said that we could change people or situations just by the energy we give out, and what you give out you get back. In a petrol station close to our house, the attendant was a rather big lady whose energy was very negative. She obviously didn't feel very good about herself. As soon as you walked in you could feel the negative vibes. Needless to say, she had no contact with any of her customers. We visited her shop at least once a week each and we would always be really friendly to her. No judgement at all. It was amazing; after only a few weeks, she totally turned and even greeted us as we walked in. This was such a change from how she was before. We showed her that we cared and were interested and that was what she gave back to us.

Who could you help by just giving them a bit more time and showing gratitude and respect, the same as you do for the people you know? Could you do that for everyone?

The best at giving unconditional love are, of course, children. Children are really good at giving you their love and, when you give them the same back, what you then receive is unbelievable. Have you ever been to a playground, a kindergarten or just with a group of children? Children can do this and so can we! Imagine that we all viewed the world through the eyes of a child and acted with child-like imagination, openness and generosity. We would connect better as human beings. Bucky Fuller said children are our elders in universe time; we have so much to learn from them as they are born in a more developed world.

When we truly connect, when we understand that everything we need is already there for us and this is how the universe is designed, magic will happen. We will find the solutions for all the challenges we face and we will live in a happier, more peaceful and stable world.

"As we express our gratitude, we must never forget that the highest appreciation is not to utter words, but to live by them."

John F Kennedy

In 1915 Ghandi returned to India to free India from the
British repression. Gandhi employed non-cooperation,
non-violence and peaceful resistance as his 'weapons' in
the struggle. Ghandi led the mass movement of millions
of Indians although he was not a political leader. Ghandi
saw a problem and realised that he could lead it by being
the difference. He connected with his fellow countrymen;
through his leadership and vision of humanity, India finally
achieved its independence.

Craig Kielburger has another great story of how, by truly
connecting with each other, we create magic. He created
Free the Children, an organisation set up to raise awareness about child labour and campaign for children's rights
across the world. In April 1995, while searching for the
comic section in his local newspaper, Craig read an article
which changed his life for ever. It was the story of Iqbal
Masih, a young boy from Pakistan, who was sold into
slavery to work in a carpet factory. Iqbal had been forced
to work 12 hours a day, six days a week, tying tiny knots to
make hand-made carpets for export. With luck on his side,
and a lot of bravery, one day Iqbal managed to escape from
his life of captivity. When Iqbal was speaking out he started to receive death threats from the carpet industry and
one day he was gunned down while visiting two cousins.

Before he read Iqbal's story, Craig had never heard of child
labour. He wasn't even certain where Pakistan was, but the
differences between his life and that of Iqbal shocked him.
The fact that Iqbal had lost his life for defending the rights
of children had a huge impact on Craig, and he knew that
he had to help. He gathered together 11 of his Grade 7
classmates and Free the Children was born. The following
year, in an attempt to focus the world's attention on the

epidemic of global child rights abuses, Craig embarked on an ambitious fact-finding mission to South Asia. In a press conference held in Delhi, India, Craig challenged the world to take notice of the stories and voices of child global debate. Craig's journey, sparked by Iqbal's heroic tale, proved that young people have the power to make a difference in the world.

Today this has grown into the world's largest network of children helping children through education, with more than one million young people involved in programs in over 45 countries.

The power of intent

In a later chapter you will read about the Intention experiment but what is intent or what is the power of your intention? It is the capacity for joy, creativity and kindness built into each of us. Wayne Dwyer says, "Intention is not something you do, but rather a force that exists in the universe as an invisible field of energy, a power that can carry us." Your intent is the power you have within yourself to make things happen, to allow the right opportunities for you to come your way. It is your intent which makes all the great things happen for you, tapping into our collective consciousness.

Chapter 3 We need to become connected again

Chapter 4

We can all make a difference

"The meaning of life is to give life meaning."

Ken Hudgins

We can all make a difference. We have heard it so many times. Make a difference, be M.A.D., be the change. How do you do it? Often we make a difference in people's lives without even realising it. It doesn't have to be the big things you do. I said earlier it can be the little things like helping your neighbour or running a club for children on a Tuesday afternoon. These things can make a huge difference in somebody's life. Often when you hear someone's life story and ask what made the difference, people tell you it was a special teacher or the neighbour who brought them to football lessons or a family member who set up his own small shop.

In this age of celebrities and consumerism, we often forget that the most important moments in our life are when we really connected with each other and are there to help somebody else.

Making a difference is a mindset

When you are yourself every day you are already making a difference. Your everyday actions determine the difference you make. If you want to make a difference for the climate, do you leave your car at home and use public transport? Do you participate in meat-free Monday? You don't have to do anything but make sure that your actions are congruent with your thoughts. Many people have great ideas but are not making any changes in their life. Let's say you want to help the environment and join the meat-free Monday movement; you will see that you start to enjoy it and, after such a small step, the next step will be even easier.

We moved to the centre of London a few years ago and, being Dutch, we use our push-bikes a lot. As a result, our car was parked on the drive most of the time, only used for the weekly shop. Last year we decided to sell the car and join a joint car scheme in our area which is brilliant. We haven't missed the car, it saves us money and the car scheme works perfectly. We help the planet and, more importantly, it has slowed our life down, making journeys together more fun.

There is a great video with Buckminster Fuller where he talks about the final exam. The final exam for humanity is about the ultimate tool: our mind. Bucky argues that we have all the solutions within us, in our minds. Our mind is the most wonderful tool we have. The way we use our collective mind over the next 10 years will determine what happens to our planet and the people living on it. Will we use our minds well enough to come up with the right solutions? We have the capability to do so.

When Barack Obama came to power his campaign was based on Change. The 'Yes We Can' slogan became very popular and relied on the fact that, together, the people of America could make a difference. People were empowered to organise events, fundraising and gatherings together and to create change within their community. Obama communicated really well that everyone had to do their own bit in order to make America a great country for all of them to live in and see the changes they wanted. The results were a staggering three million online campaign donors, 15 million registered email list members and over five million friends on 15 social networking sites. Connecting with the people of America worked and created a historical force for good.

We can all make a difference in our own way; find the way you want to make a difference and follow it. Nothing is crazy or out of bounds. The most unlikely ideas now will often become the biggest success stories. If I had said to you a few years ago, "I am going to make miniature castles out of plastic to put in fish bowls," you would probably have advised me not to give up my day job just yet. However, they are extremely popular now, and out of what seemed a silly idea, someone has made good money and made quite a difference.

Earth Hour has always been a great example for me. In 2007 in Sydney, a group of people came together and they wanted to do something about climate change. They were concerned; they realised, however, it was very difficult to get the public involved as many believed changing a light bulb doesn't make enough of a difference. So why do it? Earth Hour was set up in 2007 and the idea was to raise awareness by switching off our lights all together for one hour only, on the last Saturday of March. In 2007 two million people in and around Sydney turned off their lights for one hour. Massive media coverage was generated and people started talking about it, just through lots of people doing a small thing. As a result, they became more aware and they are each doing more things now to help the climate, also understanding that small things count. In 2008, almost 45 million people took part globally and in 2009 over 450 million people took part all over the world, making a huge difference which started from a small group of individuals coming together.

Extraordinary Ones, the company I founded, is set up along the same principles. Imagine that we all help somebody who is hungry every time we buy a meal for ourselves. At just 20 cents it makes no difference to us but it changes somebody's life. These little acts can transform the world by sharing what we have with someone else who doesn't have what you have. 20 cents = Small Change – Big Difference.

"Never doubt that a small group of thoughtful, committed individuals can change the world. Indeed, it's the only thing that ever has."

Margaret Mead

Both stories above are based on the principle 'from the power of one to the power of many'. We only need a small group of people to make a change for the rest to follow. Marianne Williamson talks about 11%. Are you part of the 11%? Personally I believe we need an even smaller group of people to create lasting change. Maybe just 2% or 5% of influencers to adopt a new idea, a new way of thinking, attitude or fashion and the rest will follow. Only a few people need to wear a certain fashion item in order for many others to follow and the fashion followers will wear exactly the same. Do you remember what happened to smoking in the last decade? Numbers have definitely gone down a lot just because it is not cool any more to smoke. Eating meat is going the same way; a small group of us are now vegetarian, many eat less meat and I reckon within five years our consumption of meat will be totally different from what it is now just because a small group of people stood up and took a stand.

Look around and see what you can do in the world around you and start with that. Are you already making a difference? Look around and see how you can improve your game. Think bigger. When you start to play a bigger game, make a bigger difference, the world around you will expand.

Find your purpose

"The future depends on what we do in the present."

Unknown

Purpose is central to good human life. Helen Keller wrote that happiness comes from fidelity to a worthy purpose. Pursuing a career, raising a family and creative vocation are all long-term goals for all cultures. Modern spiritual philosophy sees the purpose in life as improving the environment and world conditions for all beings. In the most immediate sense, this means each individual finding the special talents which are a gift to serve others. From a biological point of view, the purpose of evolution is the progression of genes. However, this is not necessarily the same thing as a human being's purpose, according to

Dan Millman in his book *The Life You Were Born to Live*.
He states that purpose is something that 'grows up in the
universe'.

In Eastern philosophies, it is more a collective goal than
an individual one. Buddhism seeks the highest level of joy
and, when you find your special talents and serve others, you will live a life of joy and highest happiness. In
the film *The Pursuit of Happyness*, Will Smith is looking
for a career for himself so he can give his son a better life
and education. The strength of the story is not just in the
brilliant acting but in the power of the story. The relentless
energy Will Smith's character finds to pursue his dream, it
is his purpose. No matter what happens, he follows it and
he succeeds.

Finding your purpose is very important to be the person
you want to be and to make the difference you want to
make. As we saw earlier, many people believe they don't
know what their purpose in life is. A 30-minute one-to-
one coaching session with someone who cares should
solve this immediately. What I often find is that people are
too afraid of stating their purpose because there is always
a 'reason' why they can't pursue it. When the universe
gives you a dream, it always gives you the tools and opportunities to fulfil your dream. You never have a dream or
purpose which you can't fulfil. So people who don't know
what their purpose is need to look inside and allow themselves to explore what it is and believe they can do it. The
only thing you need to do is to give yourself permission.

"Our deepest fear is not that we are inadequate, our deepest fear is that we are powerful beyond measure."

Marianne Williamson

As I mentioned in one of the earlier chapters, you know your purpose when you are a child and one day in your life it will come back to you. John Wood had a very good job at Microsoft in 1998 when he took a vacation that changed his life. What started as a trekking holiday in Nepal became a spiritual journey and then a mission: to change the world one book and one child at a time by setting up libraries in the developing world. On his return, he left Microsoft with only a loose vision of the change he wanted to bring to the world.

John combined business practices and the world of not-for-profit to create Room to Read, which is a network of over 7,500 libraries and 830 schools throughout rural and poor communities in Asia and Africa.

Room to Read is a wonderful organisation, building a public library infrastructure to help the developing world break the cycle of poverty through the lifelong gift of education. What a difference John is making, just because he connected with his purpose on a holiday and dared to follow his dream.

I find the story of Jacqueline Novogratz amazing. Jacqueline is the founder of Acumen, a non profit-making global venture fund that uses entrepreneurial approaches to solve the problems of global poverty. Acumen seeks to prove that small amounts of philanthropic capital, combined

with large doses of business acumen, can build thriving
enterprises that serve vast numbers of the poor. Acumen
has done a fantastic job in the last few years. Jacqueline left
a high-profile banking job to undertake a project in Africa.
As a child, she had a favourite blue sweater which she wore
until it was very old and too small, then her mum gave the
sweater away to charity. Years later, on a trip to Africa she
saw a young boy wearing her sweater. She couldn't believe
it, the name tag was still in the back. Her book is called
*The Blue Sweater: Bridging the Gap between Rich and Poor
in an Interconnected World*. Someone like Jacqueline, who
understands the world that well, will always make a big difference. What a great example of serendipity! A beautiful
word as well – Serendipity: good luck in making unexpected and fortunate discoveries. We all have examples in our
life of serendipity; my best story is probably the one of the
Kupu Kupu foundation in Bali.

On a trip to Bali in 2009, I had to organise the launch of
XLnation with Michelle Clarke. The theme of the day was
'The Awakening of the Butterfly'. We were given three days'
notice to organise an event for 200 people and we hadn't a
clue what we were going to do. Michelle looked to me for
ideas which she could then run; I said, "Let's take a break
and something will show up." We went to Ubud to shop
for a present for my son's birthday and for inspiration. As
our driver dropped us off we started walking and, all of a
sudden, I 'heard' in my head the word 'kite'. A few yards
further on, we saw a shop with lots of kites and we went
inside. Only when we were inside, we saw that all the kites
were butterflies. What a coincidence. The shop was set up
by Begonia Lopez who founded the Kupu Kupu foundation which means 'butterfly'. Begonia learned on holiday in
Bali that there are no services for handicapped people in

Bali so she decided to do something about it and established a school where she teaches handicapped children and adults so they can start to look after themselves. Even in a place like Bali, handicapped people are socially excluded. Begonia has done wonderful work since. The children of Kupu Kupu came to our event and made beautiful butterflies for us to fly, celebrating the launch of XLnation. It was truly magical, a real example of serendipity.

Children are really good at this, they have the ability to set things they like or wish for in the most unexpected ways. We should encourage them to believe and let these 'accidents' happen to live the most wonderful life.

Our son is especially good at this and it is a pleasure to see how everything he asks for every time shows up in his life in the most unexpected ways. A friend of mine, Guy, had a dream since he was a child that one day he would set up a big company with his brother to do something extraordinary – a company which does things in a way that has never been done before. A force for good in two ways: externally by helping others and internally through self-development. He founded Champions Club; the vision was for the site to build a community of like-minded individuals who would share beliefs and values – an organisation that would make a real difference in the world. Two years ago they realised it was the right time to start. Guy and Mark came together and started to share their dream with many others. Because Guy shared his message and purpose, people bought into it and joined. Now there is a great leadership team and the company will launch this year. Champions Club will be a huge success because Guy is true to the vision he has had since he was a child to make a difference for everyone. I have seen Guy work and his commitment to make a difference and for Champions Club to succeed is amazing because nothing can stop him from pursuing his dream.

When you have found your purpose, there is nothing that can stop you. Do you think Obama worries when somebody criticises him? He wouldn't be able to do his work. He simply wouldn't be a politician if he didn't feel strongly that this is what he has to do. It is not about Obama, it is about something a lot bigger than him. Nothing can stop him. Mahatma Gandhi led the non-violence movement in India and a few times he took a stance and went on hunger strike in order to try to stop the violence. Do you think he was worried and wanted them to stop fighting so he could eat? It wasn't a matter of stopping the violence just then so he could eat. Gandhi lived a life of non-violence; he wanted violence to stop for ever. His purpose was much bigger than himself and his actions showed that.

What is your purpose, what can you do that is bigger than you?

Jeremy Gilley conceived an idea for one day when all countries vowed not to wage war; a worldwide ceasefire, a non-violence day. A big dream, he wanted a UN resolution to support him. In 1998 he started talking to students, NGOs, heads of state and the UN. Jeremy was living in his mother's spare room, using it as his office at the same time. Through relentless campaigning, travelling and meeting people, he slowly gained a lot of support. He succeeded in 2001 when the resolution was unanimously adopted to establish the first ever day of global ceasefire and non-violence, fixed in the calendar as 21 September annually.

For years, Jeremy spent his own money during his crusade and he has been extremely successful. Peace One Day is a recognised charity. Now they have even managed to get Puma and Adidas working together on a peace project. Jeremy's vision has brought millions of people closer together as he had a vision: Peace. What could stop you achieving such a big purpose? Never did he let anything stop him and he succeeded. Millions of people now mark 21 September as Peace Day.

Do small things and you make a huge difference

We are all inspired by the people who have big stories to tell, who make a big difference, people with big and bold ideas. Yes, they are very inspirational, although often it will make you feel that they are so big you don't know where to start or that you don't have the skills, time or resources to achieve the same kind of goals as they have. Guess what? My advice is always just to start and do what you can do at the time. When you live a life of purpose, the universe always gives what you need when you need it. You don't even need to figure it out.

William Kamkwamba; The Boy Who Harnessed the Wind is the extraordinary true story of a Malawian teenager who transformed his village by building electric windmills out of junk. William was not attending school because his family couldn't afford the fees. There were many droughts in his area and his family's maize farm was having problems. One evening, he saw a windmill in an old library book and he set out to build one from junk. When he realised it could help provide the necessary electricity that could be a defence against hunger, he thought 'Maybe I should build one for myself'. "Many, including my mother, thought I was going crazy," he recalls. "They had never seen a windmill before. I got a few electric shocks climbing the windmill," says Mr Kamkwamba ruefully, recalling his months of painstaking work. Out went the paraffin lanterns and in came light bulbs and a circuit breaker, made from nails and magnets off an old stereo speaker, and a light switch cobbled together from bicycle spokes and flip-flop rubber. Before long, locals were queuing up to charge their mobile phones. His story got picked up by the international press and he was invited to write a book, speak at a Ted conference and is feted by people like Al Gore. By trying to help out his family, building a windmill without ever seeing one, he is now an example for a generation in the West and in Africa.

Jack Davis is an 11-year-old Florida boy who is working to have a local law changed to enable restaurants to feed the homeless, rather than throw out all their left-over food. Jack may only be 11 but that didn't stop him from having a pretty grown-up idea. When he saw something that he felt needed to be changed, he went about finding ways to change it. Jack learned that Florida restaurants throw out food that could be given to the hungry and the homeless because the restaurant owners could be sued if anyone who ate the food became ill or developed food poisoning. "I thought it was such a waste to see all this food being thrown away every single day, and I realised I could make a difference by trying to change the law," he said. Jack's idea was to pass a law that would give restaurant owners some protection from lawsuits. He got his dad to float the idea to some Florida legislators and they loved it. Now it looks like Jack's idea will become law. At 11 years old, Jack Davis is being the change he wants to see in the world.

"People do not decide to become extraordinary, they decide to accomplish extraordinary things."

Edmund Hillary

Do you believe a small thing like paying 20 cents or 20 pence makes a big difference to us? No it doesn't to us, it is small change. By paying 20 cents extra every time you buy a meal, that 20 cents is enough to give a meal to somebody who is hungry. That 20 cents could be used to help that person and his family to come out of hunger. 20 cents from you wouldn't make a difference to you and wouldn't make a difference to the world. But when many of us are connected and we all do it? Did you know that London alone serves more than three million meals in all its restaurants together every day? Imagine for every meal sold we contribute 20 pence. Together, London alone would help three million people every day. Now imagine that number globally and what we can do for world hunger. That is what small actions can do when we really connect with each other.

Isn't it a powerful thought that you could help someone else eat every time you eat?

What is your legacy going to be?

"Legacy is greater than currency."

Unknown

What is your legacy going to be? What do you want to be known for? It is not your money which people remember after you have gone. It is the impact you have made, the difference you have made that people will remember. Would you like to leave a legacy which lasts just a year after your death, 10 years, 50 plus or maybe even 500 years?

Think for a minute about people you know who passed away more than 10 years ago. Why are they being remembered? Was it a great football player, John F Kennedy, John Lennon, Martin Luther King, a local hero or maybe Mother Teresa? All people who stood up for something and followed their dream and made a difference, inspiring thousands of others.

Take a few minutes and write an article which will be printed a year or 25 years after you have died. The article is about you, what will it say? What did you achieve in your lifetime? You can create it now and have the time to make it a reality. You create your legacy. In the article, you can let other people talk about you, what they thought about you, the difference you made in their life. I did this exercise a few years ago and it is very powerful. Think outside the box, we know we all have the power to achieve. It was at a time of my life when I really set out to become truly myself and started to live a life of purpose. Thinking about my legacy, what I leave for my children, has definitely upped my game as I was playing too small.

The best master to teach you about your life's purpose and legacy must be Dr John Demartini; if you haven't heard about John, check him out. John was born in 1954 in Houston, Texas. He wore hand and leg braces to correct a birth defect. At school he had difficulty reading, writing and speaking which was later diagnosed as dyslexia, and a speech impediment. In first grade, his teacher announced to John's parents that John would never read, write, communicate, never amount to anything or go very far in life. At the age of 14, John Demartini left school and headed for Hawaii where, at 17, he had a near-death experience as a result of strychnine poisoning. These early challenges set the scene for a remarkable transformation in his late teens. At 17, a high school drop-out, unable to read or write, he met an elderly man called Paul Bragg who was able to catalyse a profound transformation by assisting him to awaken to an inspired vision of becoming a philosopher and a teacher.

John Demartini made a commitment to dedicate his life to the understanding of universal laws as they relate to maximising human awareness and potential. With focus and determined effort, he gradually broke through his dyslexia and mastered reading and writing. Then progressed to the University of Houston where he completed his Bachelor of Science degree in 1978. He has spent over 36 years avidly researching more than 270 different disciplines such as psychology, cosmology, economics, sociology, biology, theology and philosophy. Just as Paul Bragg had inspired him to break through his perceived limitations, he dreamt of being able to do the same for others. Now that is a story of change. John's vision is to empower one billion people through his programs and the education centres he sets up.

We live in a time when things are changing. Most of us realise that there is more to life that we need to make a difference. Walden University in the US is the first to set up a degree in doing good to assist students – a first of its kind and I am sure many will follow.

"What you leave behind is not what is engraved in stone monuments, but what is woven into the lives of others."

Pericles

Your legacy will always be the boldest actions you have taken in your lifetime. John F Kennedy will always be remembered for a few things. His boldest move was when he said in 1960 that within a decade there would be people on the moon. Maybe you don't need to know exactly now what your legacy will be, it can change over time. Bill Gates started Microsoft with some friends and their bold vision was: a computer on every desk. Now, more than 30 years later, Microsoft is one the biggest companies in the world and makes software, not computers. Bill Gates has set up the Bill and Melinda Gates Foundation and they are doing amazing work. It wouldn't surprise me if Bill's legacy for the foundation he has set up will be greater than for the work he did with Microsoft. The same goes for Bill Clinton. The Clinton Global Initiative is doing wonderful work all over the world and brings together many companies, governments and people creating change. Bill's work with the CGI has already given it a lot of credibility and will leave a greater legacy than what he achieved as President.

Now what will my own legacy be? I believe that nobody should go to bed hungry; food is a right for everyone living on this planet. I hope that Extraordinary Ones will help globally to empower people to come out of poverty. The way we do this is every time you buy a meal you help someone else who is hungry. Extraordinary Ones can raise millions by collaborating with others. We share what we have together. My legacy will be that I will be remembered for setting up Extraordinary Ones which has helped to end world hunger and poverty by 2025. I will have inspired many people through my views and ideas and will have helped many people to follow their own vision and live a life of purpose. I hope to be part of a legacy where humanity has come together and we have ended hunger and poverty in the world and we are having a net impact on the planet. Adding to Earth, not taking from it and thereby restoring our beautiful home. We collectively leave a legacy where we as humans are truly connected again and our hearts are open to each other. Times where we have used our collective mind consciously in the best possible way and together we will pass Buckminster Fuller's final exam.

Chapter 4 We can all make a difference

Chapter 5

Giving serves your own needs

In Africa they use the word Ubuntu. Ubuntu is a beautiful word meaning: I am because you are. Ubuntu stands for living a life of service. Desmond Tutu and Nelson Mandela live their lives in the principles of Ubuntu.

"God has given us two hands, one to receive with and the other to give with."

Billy Graham

When you open your hands to give something to someone, it is exactly the same movement as when you open your hand to receive a gift from someone. Just as we saw earlier, the emotion in your mind attaches to when you feel the heartbeat in your throat. It can be fear or it can be excitement. When we open ourselves up to give to others we are also open to receive. When we don't want to give or share, we close ourselves and are not able to receive from others. You can see that in our body language: folded arms, body turned away. In order to give or receive you need to open your hands; when you hold on to things you close your hands, they turn into fists, and we know what that stands for.

Being open to receive and to give means not just sharing with others; it means that you feel part of that community or group, family, friends or colleagues. Being open doesn't just mean receiving gifts; it also means receiving love, attention, care and communication and everything else you need in life. Receiving and taking are two totally different things; when you hold on to something because you feel it belongs to you, you close yourself off. You stop flow; you stop receiving because you are holding on. Nothing flows between you and the other person. When that happens we feel disconnected, lonely, not part of a bigger group. It is what Mother Teresa calls 'poverty of the heart'. Let go. Lose ballast and you enrich your life.

Giving can come from random acts of kindness you do for others. Often unplanned, you can do acts of kindness every day; there are opportunities all the time. Some people call it 'pay it forward' and you will see that, when you start living in his way, amazing things start to happen to you. Opportunities, gifts or just nice situations will show up in your life.

Taking is something entirely different; taking is about ego, when you live in a world of lack and when you believe that you need more in order to survive or to live. Taking happens when you are disconnected; it stops flow and happens mainly in our western world when we think we are allowed to have more then others.

Giving expands you

The way we see the world is a mirror image of the way we feel about ourselves. The thoughts we have we project out to the world. In the universe, our thoughts are real things and they will happen.

Take a time in your life when some specific things happened to you and think how that made you feel. This could be when you first got married, a new job, your child being born, the start of your business or when you lost your job, a divorce or bereavement. Remember how you felt at the time and how everything else in your life felt at the same time. In good times, everything else must have felt better, happier, more exciting and challenges felt less difficult, easier to get everything done, easier to move around traffic etc. – you get the feeling. It is a simple rule: what you see is what you get and what you appreciate appreciates. Start to live in that way, see what happens and enjoy it.

"If you wanna make the world a better place take a look at yourself and make a change."

Michael Jackson

Lynn McTaggert has spent years on the Intention Experiment. She has researched intensively if our intentions can actually change outcomes. The Intention Experiment is a series of scientifically-controlled, web-based experiments testing the power of intention to change the physical world. Thousands of volunteers from 30 countries around the world have participated in Intention Experiments so far. Can our intent, our mind, create the outcomes for us, whatever we want? The experiment achieved incredible results, especially visible in the tests they did with water. When water freezes it turns into millions of crystals. The crystals take on the most beautiful and stunning shapes and forms. It was discovered that the crystals' shapes differ depending on the circumstances. When you freeze dirty water, for example, the crystals will take on not very nice shapes, they are not coherent or symmetrical, quite simple forms really. An experiment was done where small groups of people were asked to concentrate on a bottle of water and think of a certain emotion: love, pain, happiness etc. The bottles were then labelled and frozen. The results were unbelievable; the most beautiful and amazingly-shaped crystals came up with the emotions like love and happiness. More negative emotions produced not so nice or even mis-shaped crystals. Lynn has done other experiments with water, germination and peace. Each time the results are impressive and prove that our collective intent has a huge influence on the results we get.

"We all have a gift to offer, even a smile or kindness is a gift."

Unknown

Water is a very important part of our life and we ourselves are made up of 78% water. If intent and emotions influence water in such a way, what do you think it does to us and our bodies?

If you give to other people, you attract the desire in them to give back to you. It is interesting how this works. Let me explain. The best way to get more energy is to become active and exercise more. When you are interested in others, they will also be interested in you. In nature, the purpose of each plant is to serve other plants and, by doing that, it creates a beautiful life for itself. We do know these things but does our ego sometimes get in the way?

Love is the key

I firmly believe that love is the key to everything we do. This is probably best expressed in the love a parent has for its newborn baby. There is unconditional love. A child is probably the purest form of love between two people. My mum used to tell us all the time, "Love is the only thing you can keep giving away without ever running out." Basically there is always enough love, so why don't we start to share it, hand it out; what is holding you back? We have been told to hold on to it. Pass it on and let the magic happen. Remember it always comes back to you.

"The only treasure in this life we live is in the measure of the love we give."

Cliff Richard

Research has shown that poor people give more to the community or other people in need than people with more money and resources. These are incredible results; people with fewer resources know that they have to rely on each other and understand that, by helping each other, they will be helped as well.

Imagine that you live your life in the same way you give love to your family and loved ones. Extend your love to everybody around you, be open, appreciate and acknowledge others and don't judge. When you truly open up and love and appreciate others, other people will give you that same feeling back.

"And in the end, the love you take is equal to the love you make."

The Beatles

And don't forget gratitude. Be grateful for your life, the people around you and what happens in your life. Every night make a gratitude journal and write down what you are grateful for. It works in exactly the same way and does what works best for you. Start with one thing and build it up as you see the results.

Use your wealth

With wealth building we focus too much on money. Wealth is everything you have left after you have lost all your money. I love this explanation and it is so right. Nobody can ever take your real wealth away from you. So that is the wealth you should be building all the time and the rewards will follow. Use your wealth to work on your bigger purpose.

Your wealth can be everything from your education to your experience, contacts, life challenges, your interest, your hobbies, courses you have done, your fitness. It all adds up and none of it can ever be taken away from you. It is what makes you unique.

When I was learning more about these teachings with some mentors at a program called EBS Masters in Bali 2008, the following question came to me: how could I use my wealth to work on my purpose? I knew that food was my life and my bigger purpose is: nobody to bed hungry. Make sure you spend time so that you get to know your higher purpose is exactly right, work on it and keep refining it. If there is a tiny bit of doubt within you, that means you are not there yet, you can make it better. Give it chance and it will come to you. Make your purpose so strong that every cell in your body resonates with it and you feel a really strong desire when you talk about it. You are sure that nothing can stop you; this is what you will make happen.

So how could I apply my wealth to fulfil my purpose? The first thing I did was to make a promise that I will spend the rest of my life fulfilling my purpose. Nothing can stop me. One of the mentors and I spoke about the fact that we all have certain characteristics that come with us when we are born. You can fight them or work with them, the choice is yours. All of a sudden, many struggles I had in my life became clear, what I tried to fight and the things I kept attracting into my life. On that famous plane journey home, I promised myself that things would be different from then on. I realised that I could achieve what I wanted so I would spend all my time from then on doing just that. Spend all my time doing what I enjoy and am best at. Guess what? Things started to shift from that day. It was like starting my life again. I already realised that everything I had built up in my life, my wealth, had prepared me to achieve my higher purpose. True, we still had our challenges but they became easier in the way we dealt with them. Everything I do now is measured along my goal, my purpose. If it doesn't help me to achieve my purpose, I am not even going to do it. Remember you grow by what you say no to. As I started to gain momentum, share the message, the right people showed up at the right time. The universe always knows best. Sometimes you wonder about the events which occur or the people who show up in your life or when promises towards you are not met. Always look inside and see why you are attracting it; it is always in you, everything – you attract good and bad.

Ron, the mentor in Bali, also taught me to work with my less strong characteristics, not against them. Accept them – that was really powerful because I spent so much time trying to improve areas which weren't my strengths and not really getting anywhere. This can make you frustrated, ending up feeling like a Don Quixote fighting windmills when you should be spending time enjoying what you are best at.

So how can my wealth help my purpose? I have told you that my initial thoughts were I didn't have the right skills to become a social entrepreneur. How wrong I was; everything I have done in my life has prepared me to do what I am doing now. Doing good, making a difference, becoming a social entrepreneur – just allow yourself to become one.

Are we just measuring wrong?

We have seen what wealth means and money is just one measure. When we talk about others, we often hear how many houses they have, which car or the level of their salary. Businesses are measured along the increase in turnover or their profit margin. Banks give you credit ratings which really mean how much debt they can load on to you. So we see how much money somebody is worth.

What if we are just measuring wrong? What if we have a different measure?

Imagine that at the end of the month you wouldn't just get a credit card statement; every month you'd see the positive impact you have made. For example, you have fed 10 children, given water to 100 people, 60% of the food you bought was organic and you reduced your carbon footprint by 15%. I believe that it would be really cool to see that on a monthly basis; it would easily push us to try to achieve more and together achieve the world we want to live in. Would that not connect us more?

We can take that a step further: the amount of random acts of kindness you have achieved. How do you rate on the scale of happiness how social you are? You can already calculate your value on social networks. Businesses would give out statements of their positive impacts which would go much further then the empty CSR reports which we get from many now. Imagine we are all rewarded for the impact we make. Even our tax system is measured just on the money we make. The tax system actually stimulates huge profits and rewards when you make more by taking more. Sure, you pay more tax but the net result is for the company despite the effects it has on our community or people. You know the examples I am talking about: oil companies, banks, financial services, big industries, car manufacturers, the agri-food industry but also a lot of smaller companies. It would actually help the transformation to electric cars, organic food, green energy and many more. Although there are small tax advantages when you install solar panels or energy-efficient boilers and some other initiatives, wouldn't it be better to have a tax system where the biggest polluters, the companies who take most from the planet rather than adding to it, pay the most tax? A complicated issue which needs to be explored further for us to come to a good system in order to ensure we empower people to really want to improve our planet.

"If you think you are too small to have an impact, try going to sleep with a mosquito in the room."

Anita Roddick

Would that not focus us on higher goals? Would that not focus us on our interconnectedness? Change our paradigm again? We shouldn't need to be pushed by taxes but it might help to get everybody involved in making a difference. When we have focus, we have drive. Focus means you put all your energy in one place to achieve something. A good example is in martial arts where you are taught a technique to break a wooden board or concrete slab with your bare hand. When attempting that challenge you need a great technique. The focus is not on the board but on a point far beyond that board. If your board was the focus, you would never break it. The same applies to our goals: set them higher than you want them to be, this way you always reach your initial target easily. If you don't reach your focus point, you will still break the board.

In Extraordinary Ones we measure our success by the impact we make. All our goals are set by the amounts of money we raise, the number of restaurants and consumers who join or campaign. Even with the investor who made it possible for Extraordinary Ones to expand, we agreed on the amount of money we set out to raise. So we are measured by the amount of donations going to the causes we work with; we effectively measure the impact we have on solving hunger.

When you are looking to buy something or find a new supplier, wouldn't it be great to choose them on their impact charter? You want the right product, but when you know the company not only has the product you want but also leaves a great net impact on the planet and the people, that would definitely make your choice easier, becoming a loyal customer. A real win-win as the company will get more customers.

Some countries have started to measure the happiness of their citizens, a great start I think. In the end, it will all result in newspaper headings which read something like:

North Pole ice cap has grown by x % this year and in five years it will be back at its normal level

The average temperature on the planet went down by 0.5 degrees last year

Blue fin tuna population back to 1950 level

Would that not just prove to all of us that giving back serves us all?

Chapter 5 Giving serves your own needs

Chapter 6

What food means to me

Food in the beginning

Now food plays a larger part in my life; it is not about feeding myself or being a chef and cooking for others. My purpose in life is: nobody to go to bed hungry. All my experiences, lessons and challenges in life have taught me that we all have a role to play and mine is feeding people.

You can feed people in two ways: feeding the body and feeding the mind.

Food and water are the two most basic needs we have as human beings, yet billions of us live without the security of having enough food or water to survive. Not having any food, or hunger, is a terrible thing to live with. The biggest problem many people on our planet face is not just being hungry but not knowing where the next meal is going to come from.

Mother Teresa says that there are two kinds of poverty. The first one is physical poverty which is not having food or shelter. This can always be solved. The other one is poverty of the heart, that is the one from which many people in the western world suffer. In her opinion, and I agree, this is the worst one. Feeling lonely, not feeling loved or wanted, not feeling supported – a feeling of being on your own. You feel that you are not connected to the people around you. How strange it may sound but this is harder to solve than physical poverty.

"I'm starting with the man in the mirror I'm asking him to change his ways."

Michael Jackson

I believe that the roots of the challenges we face as humanity are about being connected, interconnectedness or all being one. Somewhere down the line we have lost our connections with each other. In the West, we have developed a culture of wanting more; a culture of greed, a belief that by wanting and needing more our lives will become better. In that process, we have left many other people on the planet behind because we didn't feel connected to them any more. Even within our own groups, families and cultures we have lost the connections between us. Families have started to live separately; we have moved away, living in other towns or even moved to other countries. We have started to connect or disconnect from certain groups of people because they have more expensive belongings, bigger houses and different education or just because they don't like the same music.

Again, we have left many people behind in our own communities, creating lonely, disconnected people. Let's 'feed' all these people by becoming connected again and living from our hearts.

Jill Lester, the CEO of The Hunger Project talks about hunger as a metaphor. We can be physically hungry and we can have a hunger to succeed, we can have a hunger for money, success, wealth, love or certain relationships. Hungry for ... we all have our own examples to fill in here. I wish for a world where nobody is hungry for food, where we all have the same opportunities and we can talk about our dreams and goals on a level playing-field.

Hunger for any one of the examples above always pushes us on to higher levels. People who have known physical hunger and have overcome this are very strong and you will find they have the willpower to become very successful in what they do next in life. When you felt a hunger to succeed in, let's say, your favourite sport and you have achieved it, that then gives you the confidence to go on and succeed in something else, even better and quicker. Living in poverty is something we don't want for anyone and I will do everything I can within my power to help eradicate world hunger and poverty on this planet.

When I was eight years old I had a great group of friends. We went to the same school and did a lot of things together. Sports or anything physical was never my strong point as all that food took its toll. But friends support each other, right? One afternoon, we were playing football on a field close to our school. Two of my friends were taking turns picking their team. Another boy and I were very bad at football. To my astonishment, I was chosen last into one of the teams. This really hurt me; OK so I am rubbish at football but I am your best friend, why didn't you choose me over the others? On that day I remember promising myself that I would find something I could be No. 1 at. My friends just wanted to win the game, it didn't have anything to do with our friendship; I, however, saw it differently. This was an important experience for many years in my life and, looking back at it now, I realise it was the first turning point in my life I can remember and it shaped me for the rest of my life.

In the following years, I tried many things like music, cycling, swimming and hockey and, as soon as I realised I wouldn't excel in it, I gave up. In anything I did, as soon as I realised I couldn't be with the top performers, I gave up. It could be as simple as going to a meeting or being around friends; when others were more informed or better at the topic, I would give up, become quiet, introverted. I would choose not to 'compete'.

When I was 19 and at the hotel management college, I also became a DJ. This was in the days when it still wasn't paid very well. I made sure I knew everything there was to know about the music style I played and loved. I learned quickly and Friday nights at 'Ziggy's' became very popular and rewarding as I felt for the first time I was No. 1 at something. It taught me that you can excel at something very quickly when you put your mind to it. Knowing that people came to the pub just because I was there playing music was a great feeling. Probably the best job I ever had.

At the same time, I started at the college and we had to do a few weeks of kitchen training. 'No problem, I can manage a few weeks,' I thought; remember I couldn't even cook an egg! Instantly, I liked the kitchen and, as a result, I stayed in it for a long time. Intuitively I felt it was right and where I belonged. A beautiful way of the universe showing us what we need to do.

"A journey of a thousand miles must begin with a single step."

Lao-Tzu

Going to the hotel college wasn't planned; I was attending a technical college, against my parents' and teachers' advice. When I was younger I didn't know what to do; it was here all my friends went and I was very good at the subjects taught. Two years later and totally out of flow, I hated it of course; I needed an alternative as I promised my parents I would get a degree.

The hotel college seemed a cool idea; I was a DJ and used to help friends who had their own band. Not excelling at playing an instrument or singing, becoming their manager was the closest thing I could do to being a rock star. So I found myself at college with the intention of becoming a rock group manager at the age of 19. I caught the cooking bug and knew this was something at which I could excel. Quickly I learned as much as I could from my teachers, my mum, books and many of the top restaurants in our area. Food and my experiences like my career have taught me many valuable lessons: when you focus you can achieve anything you want; never ever let anyone tell you that you can't do something; have total trust in yourself and that the universe provides you with whatever you need.

So this is where I was going to become No.1; I wanted to become the best chef in Holland. A search to find something I could be No. 1 at from when I was eight and found when I was 20. Food and cooking became an obsession; I spent many hours getting better at it, being ambitious, working in the best restaurants in the Netherlands, France and England. In 1993 we opened our own restaurant and the quest to become No. 1 became even more important.

My wife's parents and my own parents ran their own businesses, so starting a business ourselves seemed the logical thing to do. The freedom of being your own boss is invaluable. We were young and believed we could do it all on our own. When you are good at something, customers will come, we believed. The real reason we started a restaurant was that we wanted to prove ourselves. My wife and I both had a strong feeling that we hadn't reached our full potential; something was missing and, by becoming the best restaurant, our ego would be sorted. Of course, at the time, the search to prove ourselves was all about ego.

Real success is inside yourself, not what other people think about you. In 1995 we had a group of the best Dutch chefs of the time eating in our restaurant for the opening of the first European Fine Food Fair. A very prestigious event and we had to show what we were capable of, how good we really were as chefs, a test to cook our best meal and to impress; we pulled out all the stops. Our restaurant was barely two years old and, at the end of a very successful night, the two top chefs at the time asked our age and said we were better chefs than they were at the same age. I was still only 28. Remember, I became a chef and started a restaurant to prove myself. When I heard that comment, something in my head switched and my unconscious mind thought I had achieved what I had set out to do.

It took me many years to figure out that my real interest as a chef changed from that day. The two people in the industry I respected most told me I was better than them, at the same age; I 'thought' I had achieved what I set out to do. It might sound strange, but unconsciously I never set out to have a successful restaurant, I just wanted to prove that I was No. 1 as a chef. So things changed after that day; it took me many years and challenges later to realise why this had happened.

We sold our restaurant in 1998 and it took me until 2001 to find a real new challenge. For two years, we worked as chef/managers in some top restaurants in Amsterdam, but the drive in cooking had left me. I didn't have the same passion for cheffing any more that I had before. I did my job very well but it was on automatic pilot; I was a master at it, after all. The drive I had was gone until I had a call at the end of 2000 to go to London with a friend to explore the market there.

We went from Amsterdam to London almost overnight to start a wholesale business selling to top-end restaurants. Milan and I saw a gap in the market for some top-quality products which were not widely available in London at the time. Immediately, I knew this was right. Being recognised as a chef was one thing, now I felt I needed to prove other things. A month after we had the idea, Sarah and I moved to London.

I was going to sell food. Achieving our goal in our restaurant was great; as my focus changed, we had many challenges, mainly financial, and selling it in 1998 was a relief. I felt I had succeeded as a chef but not as a business man. So starting up our wholesale company was about proving that I could set up a good and successful business. Again, there was a whole new challenge and new skills – selling and running a business, which I had to master. I already knew by being a DJ and chef that I could learn new things really quickly and that I have the energy to start new things from scratch. I saw our new business as a huge opportunity and we threw ourselves into it, leaving Amsterdam and moving to London.

Becoming a master at whatever you do is very important; something I feel nowadays but is very often ignored. The only way to become successful or to become a master at something is putting in the hours. The best advice I can give you is work hard. The reason for this is that when you master something, it is like second nature, you can be quicker at doing something and can see the opportunities better. It has to be like second nature. Nowadays, many people move from one profession or opportunity to the next without truly mastering the subject or the job; be an expert first and the right opportunities will come your way. When you are master at one subject or profession, it is a lot easier to master the next one. This has got to do with the level which you are at. When you become a master at something, you reach a high level and it will be easier to reach that same level in other skills you are learning. But make sure you choose the right industry first, one which fits your passion and skills. Mastery really means that a task or skill becomes second nature or habit. It gives you time to think and act faster. A master makes it look easy. Think of something you have mastered, like riding a push-bike. You will never forget that as your body has a memory.

I never really thought mastery was that important until two years ago, when I decided to cook for the homeless people in London at a wonderful charity called Crisis. I hadn't cooked professionally for about eight years. Still, we needed to cook for over 200 people three times a day with limited equipment and hardly any budget for the food. As you can understand, I was a bit apprehensive; I had to lead a team of volunteers but how would my skills be after all those years? The amazing thing was, as soon as I put on my chef's jacket in the morning, it all came back as if I had never been away. My body's memory sprang into action. It was wonderful and one of the best cooking experiences I have ever had for some of the most wonderful and appreciative people I know. I hope to go back many times. The experiences which I am describing to you are relevant for the lessons in my life and to where I am now as a person. I will explain these lessons in the rest of the book and how it helped me to be who I am now and my view of the world.

Food is important to us in so many other ways. We can feed the body and the mind. Food is also a way to show or hide our emotions. In our restaurant, when a customer said he didn't enjoy a dish as much as another one, I took it personally and I felt he was saying that the dish wasn't cooked well. Of course, most of the time that wasn't what the customer meant; when you go out for a long meal you will prefer some dishes more than others and some will stand out more. This strong feeling to prove myself always came from my belly; I am going to prove to you that I am a great chef and my food is outstanding, how dare you not like one of my dishes! Out of these situations, through my emotions, many of my best dishes came to life.

As a child, I remember my mother standing in the kitchen, opening a cupboard and taking some food or snacks out for herself. My mother and I shared the same love of food and the emotions around it. When there were challenges in her life, she always resorted to food saying something like, "At least I can still eat. Nobody can take that away from me." Eating made her feel better. I inherited that emotion from her and, whatever happened, I found a reason when I was younger to 'celebrate' by eating or to 'forget' an uncomfortable feeling by doing the same thing. I remember that my idea of heaven was a place where you could just keep eating all these wonderful foods without ever feeling full or getting fat. What if you could just eat all the time!

To start our wholesale business, we rented a house in Sevenoaks just outside London. Every day I went on the train with my suitcase, showing our produce to the top chefs of London. In our second week, turnover was about £110. Within two months, we had some prestigious accounts like Gordon Ramsay and Le Gavroche. From the beginning, I automatically set myself the goal to be No. 1 in our field in London, have five vans on the road and have a purpose-built unit. We started in January 2001 and achieved this at the end of 2006. We took on our first member of staff at the end of 2003; when we closed the business in 2007, we had 20 staff, five vans and a purpose-built unit very close to the centre of town. TFC Express was the best company in its field; we were known for our excellent service and the quality of our products.

With any challenges we faced, I felt that same feeling in my stomach again that I had years before as a chef. This gave me the power and energy to overcome and solve them, pushing and growing the business further every time.

Every time when you have reached your goals, it is important to set new ones immediately. At the end of 2006 we had achieved all the goals we had set for our business and we were profitable. At the same time, I met Roger Hamilton who had set up Wealth Dynamics and XL, a network for social entrepreneurs. By luck, if there is such a thing, I heard Roger speak at an event and what got me interested was when he said, "Entrepreneurs change the world, governments don't." I was in, wanted to be part of this life-changing movement, I signed up and became a member of XL. Roger became my mentor for a while; it was the start of a huge learning experience which changed my life.

One of the first things he asked me was, "What do you do in giving back?" I had to be honest and say, "Well, not that much but when we sell our business we are going to set up something for children, probably orphans abroad." Sarah and I had always had the idea that, when we sold our business, we would start something, giving to children who are not as fortunate as us. He said to me, "That is not good enough, there are many things you can do now, no need to wait." Of course he was right, we all have 'excuses' which will stop us; ours was saying "We are too busy now but when we have made our fortune, we will do good." The main thing about meeting Roger is that it had put us in contact with our real purpose in life and that we had to make our purpose our No. 1 goal. As a result, I changed my goals and I wanted to give back more, realised how fortunate I was and I started looking what that could be. A few months later, I went to Bali to one of the programs XL runs called EBS, a four-day program for entrepreneurs where you learn that business is about you and your team.

It is all about you and how you interact with others, a program I highly recommend for everyone to take part in and one of the best programs in which I have ever been involved. In one of the exercises, you learn on a 'deep' level about your past and why you are here. This was very profound stuff for me and, all of a sudden, I saw the connections between what I had done all my life and how that relates to me and my family. I realised that it is exactly the same; my story and the challenges in my life were closely connected to those of my family. I saw how disconnected I had become from so many things; it was amazing and my outlook on life changed overnight. Doing this exercise changed me for ever and making a difference became the new focus of my life.

All of a sudden, I realised that everything I had done so far was all about me proving myself. Like many of us, I had lost the connection with the people around me, the people who care about us most. This was mind-blowing stuff and I see that as one of the biggest ever changes in my life. My whole life has been about food in many different ways; my family is about food, the way we communicate, socialise and even how I deal with our emotions is all about food. I realised that that is the way I can give back to the world. My whole life, all my experiences have prepared me to make a difference through food.

This was scary and exciting at the same time. I had always looked for something to make a big difference. Previously I did it by becoming No. 1 in something, now I realised that my past, my family and my knowledge had prepared me to step up and do what I am here for on this planet: live a life of purpose. Don't forget I was in Bali with 150 truly inspirational social entrepreneurs. I also realised I had lost the connection with myself. The industry we were in shows little integrity or values; I was becoming increasingly unhappy in our own business. We had achieved the goals we set out to achieve, we were No. 1; I had built the business on being inventive and looking for opportunities. Now, as an established business, it was more about running the team and procedures, something which is totally out of my flow and not my natural way of doing things.

I said earlier that food is often allied to our emotions. My mother used to eat when she didn't feel comfortable and I got that from her. Over-eating or under-eating has to do with the way we feel about ourselves or how we think others perceive us. We all know the foods we like best; we call them 'comfort foods'. Foods you have grown up with and take you back to a certain situation, often in your childhood. It is the meaning we give to it. Children can change their mind over food in an instant. My daughter loved bananas when she was younger and would eat as many as we allowed her to eat. One day, she decided she didn't like bananas any more and she hasn't touched one since. To me it shows that everything only has the meaning we attach to it and we can change that in an instant if we want to. Let me give you an example. When you can feel your heartbeat in your throat, what does that mean? Think about it – is that fear? Is it excitement? Let me put it this way: when we decide to go bungee jumping, standing on the platform most people would feel fear. The rest would be excited to jump off a bridge with just a rope attached to their feet. The emotion you attach to that feeling is something you can change, and very easily. So you can just decide that bungee jumping is fun and you look forward to it. However, something inside us probably tells us it is different. The same goes, for example, when you go into a room of people you don't know. Most people don't like doing that. What if you just changed that feeling and go in and just enjoy it?

So when I came home from EBS in Bali, I started looking at how I could make that big difference. I decided to find my purpose, be truly the person I need to be and enjoy it.

"People of character do the right thing not because they think it'll change the world, because they refuse to be changed by the world."

Unknown

Food for thought

So I had to find my way of making a difference through food and by connecting with people. Food connects people. For many of us, socialising takes place when we share meals, cook for each other and eat together – either at home or in restaurants – and a huge industry has been built up around this. Food and cooking is more popular than ever; just look at the amount of cookery programmes and food magazines. Our love of food not only feeds us, it is also very important as a connection with others. A love for the same flavours or recipes can create long conversations or even instant friendships. Sharing food with a friend or relative or somebody who is hungry is a very powerful experience.

As it is such a powerful experience, why don't we do it all the time? Why don't we share every meal we have with somebody who doesn't have as much as we have? Is it because we have lost that connection with ourselves?

So food is the ideal way to become interconnected, the ideal way to give back and to help others. Gradually, I realised my purpose is: nobody to bed hungry – and everything in my life had prepared me for that. I also realised that I need to step up, I cannot achieve this huge bold mission on my own. I can do it by connecting with others and by working together. I have to do that by inspiring people to take action, to encourage them to see that, if I can do it, anyone can. The first step was to write my book and now to use every opportunity to speak about it and share my message.

The title of this book, *Feeding People*, isn't just about food. We can solve hunger by ensuring that everyone has enough to eat but, more importantly, by giving people a hand up, not a hand-out. Empower people to come out of poverty and end hunger themselves. I do that by telling you my story and inspiring you to connect and take action. That is why I say I 'feed people'.

Chapter 6 What food means to me

Chapter 7

Food as a right

"Extreme poverty can be ended, not in the time of our grandchildren, but our time."

Jeffrey Sachs

In 1948 The United Nations accepted the universal declaration of human rights, this in order that all human beings, regardless of cultural, organisational, religious or ethnic associations, should be entitled to certain social, political and legal rights. Much great work has been done since in that respect, although we all recognise that there is still some way to go. Amnesty International is the leader in this field. Yet we allow that many millions of people don't know where their next meal is going to come from. Doesn't everyone have the right to food on this planet? We have decided that it is all right for us in the West to have food in abundance, waste about 30% of our food and have production methods which are more harmful to the environment than cars. Yet one billion people live on less than $1 a day and go to bed hungry every night.

How can we let this happen? I believe that food should be a basic right for each and every person living on this planet. We do have enough food to feed everyone and we have the solutions to the challenges we face. What stops us? Is it that some of us believe that we should have more than others?

Why we need to solve hunger in the world

Let's just remind ourselves of a few of the statistics. Two billion people live on less than $2 a day. Over one billion people live on less than $1 a day and they go to bed hungry every night. Every four seconds a child dies because of hunger. According to the UN, it costs $3 billion to feed every child for a year. The US alone spent $700 billion to bail out the banks. In 2008, $14.8 billion was spent on bonuses in the banking industry, despite the crisis. In the UK, we spent £6 billion to make the Eurostar train journey of 90 minutes 40 minutes faster. I use the Eurostar very often and agree with Bill Liao. Bill very rightly suggested we don't spend the £6 billion but instead provide free wifi on the train and every traveller with a laptop and save £5.8 billion. It would slow us down a bit and start to value what is important a bit more, instead of trying to go ever faster. Unfortunately, it wouldn't be that simple to use the bank's bail-out money or our bonuses for good causes. However, rethinking the train link investment could feed every child for two years.

People who live on less than $2 a day still have the same obligations as we do. They need to pay for schools, clothes, housing and food. It is just unacceptable that we together as humanity have accepted to let the world get into this mess. As I mentioned, the West lives in a dream, we live in a bubble. Some have woken up and we need to do something about it very soon. Irene Khan, secretary general of Amnesty International, has written a book *The Unheard Truth*. Khan argues with passion, backed up by analysis, that fighting poverty is about fighting deprivation, exclusion, insecurity and powerlessness and the answer is not just economic growth. Her main point for me is that people in poverty lack control over their own lives. Because of Irene's findings, Amnesty has taken a new direction. With much support, and also criticism, Amnesty has taken a new road which I applaud. First and foremost, we must look at all humans as equal to us and who deserve the same opportunities as we do.

"The war against hunger is truly mankind's war of liberation."

John F Kennedy

Jeffrey Sachs, author of a book called *The End of Poverty*, argues that places where there is extreme hunger and poverty are the most politically unstable areas. Hunger and poverty causes those governments to fail, civil disobedience rises, unemployment is high, disorder and conflict will happen. We can see examples of this in Darfur, Ethiopia, Somalia, Pakistan and Afghanistan, in places where people have no livelihoods, no income and are hungry. Fundamentalists will recruit their fighters and cause the kind of problems we had, for example, in Mumbai at the end of 2008. In 2008 when we visited India, in a meeting of social entrepreneurs their 'high' minister of transport told us that India had enough food in its warehouses to feed every Indian for the next two years. We were shocked to hear that. If there is enough food for everyone, why do we see so much hunger? Why are 52% of Indian children malnourished? The minister was adamant, talked about the economic growth India has seen and how well it is doing. Of course, India has done very well in many respects but there is still much hunger and inequality. There are problems with distribution, bureaucracy and the caste system. We spoke to people in very poor villages who told us about the bureaucracy they had to go through before they would get their assigned food which by law is theirs. It is their right to get that food but often, when they do finally receive the food, it is rotten or infected with insects so it is inedible. The civil servants love the power they can execute and will use it often at will. Or they don't like to give the food to certain villages or groups because they belong to a lower caste. Although officially the caste system has been outlawed in the last century, especially in rural India it is still a big problem.

Many farmers in developing countries leave their rural existence. The droughts in the last few years mean that they can't provide a living any more for their families. The hunger urges them to move to cities to find work in order to find a better life. Many end up in the slums, they are not used to urban living and find themselves just struggling to survive. The other problem is because many move to cities, it means even less food is produced and the problem becomes bigger. Of course, it is not the farmers' fault that this is happening, they are struggling to survive. The ones who stay behind do what they can and often end up cutting the last trees in order to survive.

We need to end hunger in the world as a key reason not just to give everybody the life they deserve free of hunger and poverty but also to end violence and terrorism, create political stability, economic growth, solve the environmental crisis and to achieve oneness between all of us on this planet.

Food and water are the basics we need to survive. People

who live in extreme hunger don't care about the environment around them. Their main concern is to find the next meal and they will do anything to find that.

In the West, we want ever cheaper food, every product available the whole year round. We want Asian, French, Japanese or Italian restaurants all just around the corner. We forget about seasonal and local ingredients. Every kind of meat has to be available for everyone, which means food companies have done many things to reduce costs and drive down prices to expand their markets. Our hunger for ever more food has helped to create the global food crisis we have now. Our food has an ever higher amount of fats and sugar in it, a curse which causes all sorts of health problems and makes food addictive. We are taking supplies and food from countries that need their own supplies urgently and we are increasing carbon emissions due to factory farming and transport. Kenya, for example, produces many of the green beans available in our supermarkets, while a few miles from the fields which produce for the West, Kenyans are starving. A difficult situation as the fields also provide jobs and income for the region.

We don't just have millions of people starving in the developing world. In the US and here in the UK, the divide has become bigger and we have much poverty. The power of global food companies, their search for ever more revenue and profits, has ensured that our food is even unhealthier and contains more fat then ever. We eat less and less natural food; as a result we suffer from obesity and diabetes. We need to go back to locally-produced natural food. We need to be more careful about the choices we make. We vote with our purses through the products we buy, our buying power as a whole is massive and we can make changes by the choices we make. By the food we eat, we can help solve the environmental crisis, make ourselves healthier and ensure that people who live in hunger now get their fair share. Our choices can also help many animals on the planet, like the orang-utan living in rain forests now killed by the palm oil plantations built on the often illegally burned down parts of rain forest. Several species of fish have now been killed off by the over-fishing we are doing in the seas.

The global food crisis affects all of us

"To search for solutions to hunger means to act within the principle that the status of a citizen surpasses that of a mere consumer."

City of Belo Horizonte, Brazil

The food crisis is a complicated issue. It is all about knowing the truth. The industrial agri-foods industry is very complex and is made up of multinational grain traders, giant seed, chemical and fertiliser corporations, processors and global supermarket chains. It is funded largely with public funds for grain subsidies, foreign aid and international agricultural development. The food industry is also made up of only a handful of giants who own most of the brands and thereby control what we eat. Their political lobby and power is stronger than the oil industry. The agri-foods industry in most countries is so complicated that hardly anyone fully understands it. We don't know exactly how our food is produced, what's in it, the labelling is very unclear and politicians don't have the (will) power to change it. It means that they are almost outside the law.

A recent survey in Holland showed that cornflakes contained the metal from old bicycles. Yes, really! On the packaging it tells you the cornflakes contain iron. Exactly! It sounds like a bad joke but this is a fact. The metal is very finely ground and added to the cornflakes. Of course, these metals have no positive impact on your body at all and can actually be quite harmful. I am sure there are many similar stories to tell.

What really is in our foods is staggering when you start to look into it. Labels are very unclear and don't tell the whole story. Informing customers and trying to do good also sometimes goes the other way. Basically, I am in support of the organic movement and believe it does a lot of good work, although regulations are very unclear and sometimes make it difficult for consumers and producers to understand what exactly is going on. Some food sold under the organic name is not so organic after all. On the other hand, many farmers or producers find it really difficult to qualify for the organic approval for several reasons. Sometimes it is just because their particular case or circumstances are not yet taken up in the regulations. I know of a farmer who has even stricter standards and for that reason can't be qualified – a difficult situation. The organic brand has run away with itself, hence some changes are needed to fight to get all food organic and reduce all unnatural pesticides and fertilisers.

Fish, for example, cannot be qualified organic because you can't know what the fish has eaten. Crab sticks are made of cheap white fish and egg whites. Last year in France on the supermarket shelves there was a heavily-marketed product of organic crab sticks. My first question is always "Why call it 'crab sticks' if there is no crab in it?" That basically already shows what is wrong with information on food labels (and it is allowed). When I lived in Holland, a typical product was liver sausages made from pork. The best ones are veal liver sausages. You would assume these are made of veal liver; at the time, only 10% of the product had to be made of veal liver. Why would you need to call it veal? The only reason the crab sticks could be called organic was because they were made with organic egg whites. Is this trying too hard?

The meat industry is very powerful. In the US alone, one million land animals are killed every hour – an estimated 10 billion per year (chickens, cattle, hogs, ducks, turkeys, lambs and sheep). Nearly all of them are raised on factory farms under inhumane conditions. These industrial farms are also dangerous for their workers, pollute surrounding communities, are unsafe to our food system and contribute significantly to global warming.

Global warming and the food you eat have a bigger connection than you may think. Global warming refers to an average increase in the Earth's temperature, which in turn causes changes in climate and has devastating effects on our environment and our everyday lives. Excessive greenhouse gasses in the atmosphere can trap too much heat, effectively cooking the planet and causing major problems .You can watch All Gore's movie *An Inconvenient Truth* to see the effects of global warming or find one of the many websites dedicated to this. We humans are responsible for upsetting the natural balance of heat and gases in the environment.

Agriculture emits gases in various ways. They are created just by the production, packaging and transport of pesticides and fertilisers. When applied to cropland, they cause erosion and pollute water sources.

Farm animals generate gases in several ways. Their waste is often stored in large pits which emit methane. Cattle also emit methane as part of their digestive process. After food is grown, it is packaged and transported an average of 1,500 miles.

Our lust for ever cheaper and more meat has resulted in a lot of grains and crops being used to feed animals on factory farms, taking away the food it could produce for humans and, at the same time, contributing to raising carbon emissions, more air pollution and the contamination of our ground water. The World Bank, IMF and WTO have granted subsidies to, for example, the US to sell their rice for exportation. These so-called trade linearisation regulations were imposed on developing nations. Honduras, for example, has been swamped by import surges of rice from the US since 1992. Honduras had about 25,000 rice farmers in the late 1980s; now statistics show fewer than 1,300. The people living in countries where these subsidised products come in start to buy the cheaper alternatives from abroad, thereby slowly killing their own farmers' trade which can't compete against the very low subsidised prices from abroad. As food prices rise globally, this affects the poor immediately. Whilst the growing prices might be good for the Honduras farmers, the locals will buy the local rice as the imports are getting too expensive. There is only a handful of farmers left so they can't produce enough and the poor people of Honduras are struggling as they cannot afford to pay the higher prices. The recent food crisis has seen the international community react with a high level task force dealing with the World Bank, IMF and WTO; however this takes time. It needs a review on trade policies; it is an opportunity for Honduras and many other countries with the right support to regain control of their own food production with import protection. It will take time to rebuild the land and train the farmers as many have moved to urban areas, doing different jobs or living in slums.

You can see how the environmental crisis is so closely related to the human crisis we have on our planet. The need for animal feed and the rise in oil prices has resulted in many farmers starting to produce crops for biofuels or ethanol. This is backed by governments who pay large subsidies as they rightly believe oil production has peaked and we need to look for alternatives; but these biofuels are not the right alternative.

The use of farmland to produce crops to feed animals at factory farms and the huge resources going to ethanol production have a huge impact on the food crisis we have in the world. The rising oil prices are linked directly with food prices. The price of oil pushes up the production costs of food because of the heavy loads of diesel our tractors and lorries use. The heavy subsidies and regulations for oil companies to use biofuels have convinced many farmers to produce even more biofuel and, by doing so, are pushing up global food prices. The global food reserves have declined hugely over the last few years so the rising prices have a huge effect on the local food prices in developing countries, giving the poor even more problems struggling to get their daily meal.

Ethanol is basically an alcohol. Brazilian sugar-cane ethanol has an energy ratio of 8:1, meaning that if you add up all the fuel used to fertilise, irrigate and produce it, it is eight times more efficient. You get eight times the energy you have put in. Oil has a ratio of 5:1. Corn ethanol has a ratio of 1.3:1; yes, that is all, making it almost worthless as an energy source. The US has committed to produce 36 billion gallons of biofuel by 2020. This will use vast amounts of land, although it will replace only 7% of the country's oil usage. Filling an SUV's tank with biofuel would take about 220 kilograms of corn – enough to feed one person for a year. I am all for finding new energies so we stop using our natural resources; however I am convinced that biofuels is not one of the solutions. The land could be used far better for food production. Political pressure and a $1.38 subsidy per gallon – half the wholesale price – make it a very interesting product to grow. Thanks to ethanol, the price of beef, poultry and pork in the United States rose more than 30% during the first five months of 2009. Pork farmers now find it cheaper to fatten their animals on trail mix, French fries and chocolate bars. Due to rising corn prices in Mexico, tortilla prices have jumped by 60%, leading to food riots. In many other towns, we have seen growing violence and riots because of the escalating food prices. If we don't do something about rising food prices it could mean that, by 2025, 600 million more people will go hungry. 2025 – is that not the year we are supposed to end world hunger?

The good thing is that biofuel can be made from almost any plant matter and research is being undertaken at the moment. One of the most interesting plants being developed is the use of algae as a source for biofuel, although the challenge will be the scalability.

The food we waste is another story in itself, in fact some great books have been written on this matter. In the US, households waste as much as 40% of the food they buy; in the UK is close to 33% and in Europe it is about 25%. This has many reasons: it is due to shelf-life on packaging; we just buy too much and don't know what to do with it; people of our generation often don't cook for themselves so don't know what to do with leftovers; the food simply doesn't look perfectly round, ripe enough or we don't like that shade of green. Another factor is that consumers only shop once a week and get everything at the same time from the same shop for convenience. When I was a child we shopped for vegetables a few times per week. Supermarkets demand that farmers only supply them with vegetables within very strict specifications otherwise they will not pay, as they say consumers will not buy the product. Therefore, perfect food ends up in skips, stating it is unsellable while often it is perfect.

Research has shown that the food wasted in the UK and US alone could feed the whole world three times over; these are amazing facts. Three times over. We need to be re-educated on food. We need to learn where food comes from, when it is at its best, what we can do with it and how we can use every bit of a chicken, for example, to make full use of it and reduce costs. My grandmother used a chicken to make stock as the basis for a soup and the meat was used in a creamy sauce with puff pastry – two beautiful meals for the whole family from just one chicken. It sounds simple and it is. If you look in a supermarket now, you see shelf after shelf of ready meals. I have nothing against it once in a while but it does nothing for you compared to healthy, freshly-cooked meals using local and seasonal ingredients and there is less waste and packaging.

Food waste goes through the whole chain; you can find waste at every level. In developing countries as well, much food is wasted. Often when there has been a successful harvest, there is no knowledge of preservation, how the food can be kept and stored for some to last into the leaner months in between two harvests. The Hunger Project solves this by educating farmers about saving their crops and how they can store them. In many of the epicentres they build, there is a large barn to store crops like potatoes. As many poor people are in survival mode and don't know when the next successful harvest will be, they will often eat the food within a few weeks or months. Remember the story I told you about India where there is enough food for every Indian and it often doesn't get to the people or it is rotten and infested. What an unnecessary waste, especially as so many there live in hunger. The hot and humid weather makes it extremely challenging as refrigeration is not an option. In all, food waste is a huge problem. Have a look around your supermarket and see what you find, it really is staggering, and think of the amount of waste you don't even see. It is also easy to see that we can put our resources to use a lot more efficiently.

The solutions we have available

One of the solutions to end hunger which made a big impression on me is in Belo Horizonte, Brazil's fourth largest city; 2.5 million people, 11% living in extreme poverty and 20% of its children going to bed hungry every night. In 1993 the new mayor, Patrus Ananias, declared food as a right for his citizens. He basically said, "If you are too poor to buy food in the market you are no less of a citizen, I am still accountable to you." What a beautiful statement, and I immediately thought 'imagine that we would all do just that.' A twenty-member council was set up to create a new food system for the town. They came up with dozens of innovations, especially connecting the farmers of the area and the citizens. It created dozens of choice spots or what we call farmers markets so farmers could sell directly, and it redirected the profits to the farmers and consumers. Everyone got a better deal. On retail food, profits are often 100%. It gave the poor direct access to healthy and affordable food. Income for farmers was growing and they could support themselves better in a time when, on average, a farmer's income in Brazil went down by 50%. On some basic products, they set prices at about two-thirds of market value. Top sellers at the markets agreed to go to the back streets and sell there as well. Three huge restaurants were set up, averaging 12,000 meals a day using fresh local produce, for less than half a dollar per meal. The 'food as a right' program created a real buzz which also went into local schools and communities so they could all take part.

"We're fighting the concept that the state is a terrible, incompetent administrator," civil servant Adriana explained. "We're showing that the state doesn't have to provide everything, it can facilitate. It can create channels for people to find solutions themselves."

"I knew we had so much hunger in the world. But what is so upsetting, what I didn't know when I started this, is it's so easy. It's so easy to end it."

Adriana, Belo Horizonte

Now, 40% of Belo Horizonte's population benefits from the scheme; fruit and vegetable consumption went up and infant malnutrition went down by 50%. The cost of it all is $10 million or about 1 cent per inhabitant per day.

After Belo Horizonte more cities will follow. Inner cities in America also have big problems with hunger and poverty. In July 2009, San Francisco Mayor Gavin Newsom issued a comprehensive food policy for the City – the first ever of its kind and a sweeping plan for improving food accessible in the region. The plan, which seeks to ensure that area residents are able to obtain nutritious food, is expected to increase the support of local farms, thereby impacting all of Northern California.

The policy calls for several actions. It requires that all departments audit land under their jurisdiction to find land suitable for gardening; that food sold by vendors (under city permits) meets new health and sustainability standards; that city meetings providing food make sure that food is healthy and locally-produced; and that, within two months, food the city purchases be grown regionally and sustainably. This is a major step to ensure food produced locally is healthy and is available for every citizen/consumer.

Dan Barber, the well-known American chef who grows most of the products he uses on his own Blue Hill Farm, answers the question "How can we feed the world?" with "Think about how we feed ourselves. We do produce enough calories to feed the world a few times over." He argues also that we have to look at the systems we use; factory farms, the agri-industry, feedlots or fishing farms are not the answer. The industry has been telling us for many years that it is feeding more people more cheaply; what is wrong with that? It has come with huge costs: we have taken away many things from the environment; there is animal cruelty; CO_2 emissions have risen; we have health problems like obesity; and there is potential or real extinction of many species. As a top chef, he argues that these production methods have never produced outstanding-tasting products. We need to go back to every community to feed itself and he has some great examples for it.

Normal fish farms need at least two to fifteen times the amount of protein to produce 1kg of fish and produce a huge amount of waste polluting the waters. There are better solutions. Veta la Palma is a fish farm located on an island in the Guadalquivir river, 16km inland from the Atlantic in Spain. Veta la Palma produces 1,200 tonnes of sea bass, bream, red mullet and shrimp each year. However, unlike most of the world's fish farms, it does so not by interfering with nature, but by improving upon it. The ecologically-sound practices benefit more than the farm's fish and the people who eat them. By re-flooding drained lands, Veta la Palma transformed itself not just into a fish farm but, somewhat unwittingly, into a refuge for migrating aquatic birds as well.

Looking out on to the carpet of flamingos that covers one of the lagoons that make up Veta la Palma, the fish farm in southern Spain where he is biologist, Medialdea shrugs, "They take about 20% of our annual yield but that just shows the whole system is working. Veta la Palma raises fish sustainably and promotes the conservation of birdlife at the same time." The drained lands which were not used before have proved to be an incredible natural environment for fish and wildlife which was previously totally overlooked.

Another example Dan uses is Eduard Sousa. Eduard produces ethical *foie gras*. *Foie gras* is normally produced by force-feeding ducks or geese so their liver swells up and becomes a delicacy. Eduard raises geese in Extremadura Spain for their liver but doesn't force-feed them. The 1,000 or so geese Sousa raises each year roam freely, eating their fill of acorns and olives, on a farm that replicates the wild as closely as possible. "If you convince them that they're not domesticated, their natural instinct takes over," he explains. His geese roam on land of more than 30 acres where wildlife has been replicated, even planting the necessary herbs for flavouring. Eduard's products taste delicious and win prizes all over the world.

I am not advocating the use or production of *foie gras* here at all. I believe it is an amazing story which shows we can produce in a way that suits the environment: no machines or harmful pesticides, take care of nature and we are making better-tasting products. We have the opportunity to use similar production methods for all kinds of animals. We have to be more aware of the choices we make, be it at home or having a celebratory dinner in a top-class restaurant.

Chapter 7 Food as a right

Chapter 8

You don't need a lot

I love stories where people have started companies, organisations or just followed through ideas with their ideas and passions, started with almost nothing and through determination, hard work and focus, build up something unbelievable. It proves that you don't need a lot to start and often, when starting something new, it is a hindrance to have a large amount – of either cash or resources. It can stop creativity and progress in many ways; too much money often gets spent with limited results.

A seed starts growing in the ground with hardly anything around it. It takes nutrients from the ground around itself, it finds everything it needs. As it grows, it finds enough food and water to grow more and the process continues. When we have an idea for a business, we often get caught up and find many reasons not to do it. We procrastinate. My advice is always: just start. Don't wait until you have every role in your team filled or you have enough customers. Start with what you have, the right people will always show up at the right time. Show people what you have set out to do, communicate with others what you are doing and let the ripple effect start. Most certainly, the right people to help you will show up.

The question I often get asked is "Where is the money going to come from to organise our event?" or "How am I going to find the right team, how can we pay for the venue?" My answer is "Wherever it is needed." When you follow your heart it will show up.

"We need men who can dream of things that never were."

John F Kennedy

Start and start small is always my advice. The more you work on your idea, the more it will become a reality. Work hard, as especially in the beginning that is what you need to do. As you attract more helpers and supporters, it will become easier. Work hard but also act smart and think fast. Starting small doesn't mean don't think big; I believe we should always set ourselves big goals so we always focus on a point far beyond our actual target. This is the only way to achieve the actual target. I have set the fundraising bar for Extraordinary Ones five times higher than the actual target we have agreed with our funder. Many founders of now large established companies think back very fondly of the days when they started. Virgin started on a barge in west London. Steve Wozniak of Apple says, "All the best things that I did at Apple came not having money and not having done it before, ever." Zappos, the American brand which started selling sunglasses and trainers, is mostly known for its outstanding service. Zappos has been seen as an overnight success but was four years in the making before we even heard about it. The same goes for Kiva, the platform for micro-finance which became an almost overnight success after its launch. The team behind it did a brilliant job; it also took them four years to launch. Starting up something new, especially when it has never been done before, takes time. Use that time well. It took us about a year and a half to find the right concept for Extraordinary Ones and now, six months after we had our first small launch, we still spend most of our time improving, removing all bottlenecks and making the right connections. By doing this at a slower rate, we are actually going faster, allowing the right actions to happen. We have put a lot of time and effort into Extraordinary Ones – pure sweat really, but not huge amounts of money. I have spent money on some travelling I have been doing, staying in Holland preparing meetings and other things. If we had had lots of money to spend, we would probably have launched an earlier version of our concept which would probably have failed or not been as successful as it wasn't ready, and we would have needed to spend more money getting it right. Thinking about it, the most money I have spent was on the first idea: sell food and feed a child. Buying stock, sorting packaging and hiring a warehouse cost me far more than what we have achieved so far. It stretched us and it was very challenging at times; we believe it really has brought us to where we are now: a very interesting concept with huge potential. It shows that the connections we are making at the moment are just phenomenal.

"How wonderful it is that nobody need wait a single moment before starting to improve the world."

Anne Frank

The people showing up around us now, offering their help genuinely, is something we could never have paid for or wanted to be paying for. The people we are attracting are here because they see we give first. They show up because they want to be part of it. It opens them up and they want to contribute and also give, which is very rewarding in that we have created a place where others can give their time, money or knowledge to help grow our concept.

The best example that we don't need a lot to make things happen is the story of Stone Soup. How can we make the most wonderful soup to feed a village? Start with a pan of water, fire and lots of belief and ask everybody to add just one thing. The moral of the story, of course, is that we all have something to give even if we believe we don't have anything, and when we come together and give what we have, we can make anything happen. I am glad to see this model of people coming together with an idea or plan and starting to make things happen more and more. The changing belief of more people wanting to make a difference has helped. The financial crisis has pushed many people to look at new opportunities, or it has even pushed them to finally pursue their dreams. Entrepreneurship is more popular than it has ever been. Fewer financial resources are available which has made us more resourceful and creative to find solutions. All these facts have resulted in more and more people coming together, making a difference.

"Don't ask yourself what the world needs; ask yourself what makes you come alive. And then go and do that. Because what the world needs is people who have come alive."

Howard Thurman

In the old ecology, it was all about the survival of the fittest where the strongest would survive. The central figure was the limited identity we had about ourselves, so the central figure was: Me. In the new ecology it is about survival of all of us. We have to apply our wisdom; wisdom is the science that nurtures the relationship between all of us, looking after life and nature.

What others have done?

Some of the most inspiring stories of people who had an idea and started making it a reality are stories about young people. They didn't worry if it is possible or where the money is going to come from. Young people have a lack of fear – what a beautiful feeling that is! We are born fearless; if you don't believe me, have a look at a baby. We face the biggest challenges of our life as babies and we conquer them fearlessly – like learning how to walk. We fall and get hurt and get up hundreds of times until we finally can walk effortlessly. A baby will try every attempt with the same energy and enthusiasm until it succeeds. Slowly, life steps in and we lose this lack of fear and it gets worse when we get older. What is your fear that stops you? Think about it.

What would happen if you started your business or followed your big purpose with the fearlessness of a 20-year-old? Young people have started some amazing projects because they had no fear, just belief, and made it happen.

In 2007 three Australians started a school in Kabul teaching the local youth about skateboarding. They saw this as a way to connect with the local youth; the expat life didn't allow them much opportunity to interact with the locals. Quickly, they discovered that by following their passion and asking friends back home for boards and equipment, the youngsters started to show up and wanted to take part. It connected Afghans with each other and with the foreigners, which is normally a strained relationship.

Afghanistan has the world's highest percentage of school-age children but some of the toughest conditions. Illiteracy is rife, beggars swarm the streets of Kabul and there are 600,000 child drug addicts. Just 1% of students make it to university. The national pastime is Buzkashi, where two teams of horsemen fight over a calf carcass. Dog-fighting and cock-fighting are also popular. Skateistan, as the project is called, started with 10 second-hand skateboards. Skateistan tries to be different; it started small, offering free skateboarding classes in public spaces, with virtually no budget. Now they are planning to build the city's first skate park.

Sixty-one years after Gandhi's death, his image is everywhere in India, yet his message of peace and non-violence is often forgotten. India has its fair share of violence, caste problems and terrorism. A few people had an idea to let Gandhi talk and they announced their initiative 'ingandhisshoes' on the 61st anniversary of his death. The idea is that everybody has an image of Gandhi in their wallet as he is on all currency notes. On a market square in India, they started to distribute small stickers with Gandhi's sayings on them. The stickers were put on currency notes and every time you use one of the notes, Gandhi's message gets spread and it reminds people. The message got spread in schools, markets and amongst people. It caught on, people got inspired and a petition was started to put Gandhi's message on all currency notes. I hope they succeed with their brilliant initiative, a great way to be reminded all the time of Gandhi's wisdom and how we can all play our part in it.

We often hear stories of people coming together and organising charity events raising a certain amount of money, which is all fantastic. However, it often makes me wonder if, by better use of our time, better collaboration and resources, the results could be even better. See how 11-year-old Jack Yeilding did it: he raised over $41,000 from two lemonade stands and a charity car wash. Jack raised the money for sick children in his local hospital. How Jack did it was that he has a condition himself and one day announced he would raise money. His determination, his passion and his lack of fear got others involved and, with their help, Jack raised that amount. The adults just needed a push by somebody a lot younger (with no fear) to stop every excuse and to see that it was possible. Once you get together, it is a lot easier than you think.

Circumstances or the financial crisis are not a reason to stop you from starting your new venture. Some of the biggest companies in the world have started during a crisis – in the 1920s, the 1970s or, more recently, internet start-ups which survived the dot.com crash.

In 1859, Swiss businessman Henry Dunant had a vision. He had been appalled at the suffering of thousands of men, on both sides, who were left to die due to lack of care after the Battle of Solferino in 1859. He proposed the creation of national relief societies, made up of volunteers trained in peacetime to provide neutral and impartial help to relieve suffering in times of war. In response to this idea, the Red Cross was formed in 1863. Henry Dunant also proposed that countries should adopt an international agreement which would recognise the status of medical services and of the wounded on the battlefield. This agreement was adopted at the Geneva Convention in 1864. Henry's idea was very clear and it grew very quickly because it was beneficial for everyone. We all know the magnificent work the Red Cross has done since then.

In 1978, two friends opened an ice cream shop in a renovated gas station in Vermont. Ben and Jerry combined ice cream making with social activism by creating a three-part mission statement that considered profits as only one measure of success. Their mission statement has three parts: a social mission, a product mission and an economic mission. Their social mission describes the company's need to operate in a way that recognises their influence on society, and the importance of improving the quality of life all over the world. Their product mission states that they will always strive to make the finest quality products, working to use natural, wholesome ingredients. It also states that they will advertise business mannerisms that respect the Earth. Their economic mission describes their promise to operate their company on a 'sustainable financial basis of profitable growth, increasing value for stakeholders and expanding opportunities for development and career growth for employees.' In 1980 they started to sell their ice cream in pints so they could sell to other shops. Ben and Jerry have always been very creative in their marketing, for example creating the biggest ever ice cream sundae and every year they have a free ice cream day in each of their shops. The main thing was to have fun and the flavours they have created reflect that social activism has always been high on the agenda. In 1992, Ben & Jerry's joined in a co-operative campaign with the national non-profit Children's Defence Fund; the campaign goal was to bring children's basic needs to the top of the national agenda. Over 70,000 postcards were sent to the American Congress concerning kids and other national issues. Ben & Jerry's went from a small shop in 1978 to being sold to Unilever in 2000 for $325 million whilst their turnover at the time was $55 million.

Their creativity and unique ideas for doing business meant that 98% of consumers knew their brand, although only 14% ever bought their products, hence the high valuation. Doing good and having a great business at the same time, Ben & Jerry's is a prime example for all of us.

Approximately one billion people in the world live in slums and the number is set to rise to one in three if you believe the worst predictions by UN agencies. People end up in slums for a number of reasons; urban people move to the city in order to find employment and to provide food for their family. Local authorities have little control over slums; slums are the product of failed policies, bad governance, corruption and a lack of political will. Very few countries have recognised this critical situation and very little effort is going into providing jobs or services. Slums have their own laws and gangs and crime often takes over. On the other hand, people living in slums have become very innovative at looking for answers to better their lives. In general, people at the bottom of the pyramid are extremely resourceful. Dharavi in Mumbai is the biggest slum in Asia; about 600,000 people live in an area of less than a square mile. There are around 4,500 small businesses generating over $1 billion in sales. These are enormous figures. The main activities are leather products, pottery and jewellery, selling to shops all over the world. This is an interesting feat; what is more interesting is how they do it. All the businesses are run from slums or small rundown buildings, often providing everything they need for their workers within a few feet. Their workspace, living and sleeping facilities are all very close to each other or are even in the same room. In these circumstances, people have found a way to make a living; the one thing they have to rely on most of all is each other. Living so close to each other is not easy but it also provides opportunities, as one business provides goods and services for the others next door. In the West, we don't like seeing the facilities and the circumstances under which the employees live and work. What we need to do is help and support them to increase their earnings and improve conditions rather than turning a blind eye.

An important part in any slum, including Dharavi, is recycling. Everywhere you go, you see rag pickers going through rubbish. In slums, mainly the plastic is cleaned and sorted – a tedious job finding every scrap of plastic they can reuse. From the West, we ship tons of our plastic to India where it is sorted into well over 90 different varieties. Whatever can be used again is recycled, the rest is thrown away. As shipping rates fell and more ships had empty space, more and more of our waste has ended up in India, providing work for people in slums, paying low wages and also growing their waste plastic mountain. Why ship it out to India to throw it away there? Why produce it in the first place using so much of our valuable oil? Did you know that the US alone needs 12 million barrels of oil per year just to produce its need of plastic bags? It is not right to use or produce plastic to support the rag trade abroad, making us feel good supporting with the pollution we cause at the same time. We can use the money spent in more effective and sustainable ways.

Can waste bring you the coolest start-up company? Imagine that there is zero waste. Tom Szaky believes there is no such thing as garbage and every product he sells is made totally out of garbage. In 2001, Tom started to sell worm poop in used soda bottles as an organic fertiliser; his idea was to have a company with a net positive impact. Tom's

dream was to find a new, more responsible way of doing business that would be good for the planet, good for
people and good for the bottom line! TerraCycle has won
many awards and accolades since then for its environmen-
tally-responsible business model. TerraCycle makes over
50 affordable, eco-friendly products from a wide range
of different non-recyclable waste materials. It is active in
many countries and has a turnover of millions of dollars.
TerraCycle works together with non-profits and producers
to collect waste to turn into its many cool environmentally-
friendly products.

One of Tom's biggest challenges in the beginning was to
find the screw tops for his soda bottles as he didn't want to
pay for them and they had to be waste. Whole Food, Wall
Mart, Home Depot and shopping channels now proudly
sell his trendy products. Not re-cycle but up-cycle. A great
example of how you don't need a lot to start something
new. Be bold, fearless and believe and anything is possible.

Chapter 8 You don't need a lot

Chapter 9

Business making a difference

In the last few years, we have seen the immense growth of social businesses. It is now very popular to set up a social enterprise which gives back or contributes to society. Profit used to be the driver for most businesses and now we have seen a trend of moving away from that. Doing business is a lot more than just generating profit. We talk about the three Ps: People, Planet, Profit. Many businesses do a lot of good work towards this and even more use it as a good marketing tool, selling a lot of hot air. So what is good, what should you do or what can you do with your business? Nowadays, our businesses have become more integrated with ourselves. We build our business around our passion and purpose – around who we really are, not just to make a living; it is our life. Consumers demand that your business does good, makes a difference and helps to improve our planet and the lives for all of us living on it. Consumers are more aware than ever before of what they want and what they buy. The purchasing power of consumers by choosing with their wallets is scary for some businesses but I believe it is a huge opportunity when you are not afraid of change and you are passionate about making a difference. In that respect, I like the word 'unreasonable'. Are we unreasonable to demand a better world? Is it unreasonable to believe we can end world hunger? Do we want a business with unreasonable results? Not just reasonable results. Unreasonable people get unreasonable results, achieving things others thought were impossible. In order to make changes, we need to be unreasonable; reasonable is keeping the status quo as it is now.

"The ones who are crazy enough to think that they can change the world are the ones who do."

Steve Jobs

Ethical consumers

Consumers are becoming more and more aware of the choices they make. The voting power they have is through their purses. The rise of the ethical consumer is simply the fact of spending more responsibly; we are starting to put our money where our ideals are. More and more of us are buying organic food, energy-saving light bulbs or are taking public transport more often instead of using our cars.

In a Times survey in the summer of 2009, it was revealed that 82% said they have consciously supported local or neighbourhood businesses this year. Nearly 40% said they purchased a product in 2009 because they liked the social or political values of the company that produced it. Research by Cavills Australia and Cone Inc. has shown that, of consumers: 79% switch brand when it is connected to a good cause; 65% find emotional incentives for involvement important; 85% say they have a more positive image of a product or company when it supports a cause they care about; and 86% of consumers believe businesses should be involved with causes. These are impressive figures which prove that we all feel we are becoming more conscious of the life we are living and the choices we make.

As a business, we need to use that trend and make sure we use this to our advantage. GoodBrands in the UK announced that those businesses which don't react to the current trend and give back will have difficulty attracting customers within two years.

What is an ethical consumer? We established that he or she votes with his or her purse through the choices they make and therefore don't accept willingly any more what corporates, supermarkets or simply the corner shop puts in front of them. Ethical consumers buy products which align with their values and support or give back to what is close to their purpose. Ethical consumers are well-informed, know what is going on and use several platforms like social media to communicate with each other. As a business, it is a group to consider; when you have consumers on your side they will help you grow your business and spread the word.

Every kind of business can become a social enterprise and use business skills and products to make a difference. So what can your business do?

Social entrepreneurs, business for good and conscious capitalists

There are many different explanations for the term 'social entrepreneur' or even 'social enterprise'. What does it mean? A social entrepreneur is an individual, somebody who sees a problem and creates a business around it to solve the problem. A social entrepreneur is someone who can't be stopped; his or her drive to change the world is very strong and inspires others, so not everybody will be a social entrepreneur. Ashoka's Bill Drayton explains how you can be an effective social entrepreneur; firstly, you have to give yourself permission to be one! In my opinion, social entrepreneurs are the ones who push the boat out, try to change a situation and find innovative solutions. There is nothing wrong with just being an entrepreneur and giving back through a concept, which many businesses are doing. In fact, we need as many of you as we can find. Do transactional giving, cause marketing or give a percentage of your profit, but that should simply be part of being an entrepreneur.

There are many terms for these kinds of businesses: business for good, conscious capitalist, the 1% club or you practise cause marketing. The main thing for business is to look at your purpose. What do you do, what is your mission, is it aligned to you and your staff, who you are? When you have established that, it should be as closely connected to your business as your passion and purpose is to yourself, as I spoke about in previous chapters. Passion in business is also what gets you excited in the morning and makes you get out of bed and wanting to start the day.

The more you align your giving back with your values and the purpose of your business, the better the fit and the bigger the results you will get. An accountancy firm could support small businesses in Africa, helping them with accounting and systems. I know a coaching firm in the UK whose staff travel to India once a year to spend a week doing workshops with people in small villages.

A building firm in Holland gives a percentage of its profits to Habitat for Humanity. They build houses for people who can't afford to buy them in developing countries.

As you see, there are many possibilities which I believe should become the norm.

Cause marketing happens when a business and a good cause work together and create a win-win situation, when the name of the business and cause are connected in order to raise money for the cause. One of the best examples is the RED campaign set up by Bono and some of his friends. RED partners with large companies like Apple and Starbucks. The companies sell a product under the RED brand, like the RED iPod, and a percentage of the sale price goes to combat HIV in Africa. The campaign has been very successful and has raised millions of dollars to fight HIV. The drawback is that RED is only available for large companies who can pay a lot of money to take part. I see RED as a great example of doing wonderful work; as a smaller company you need to look how you can make that work for your business.

One Tribe is a great example; they do cause marketing via T-shirts. They clearly state that, of each T-shirt, 50% goes to the related cause. So by choosing a T-shirt, you know which cause you are supporting and for how much. The designs are superb and they support causes like Grassroots soccer, Childline or Water.org. Another wonderful example is Little Feet. In 2006, Stefan Tubbs started the Little Feet campaign to supply footballs for children he had seen during a trip to Iraq as a news anchor man. Little Feet works exactly like One Laptop per Child. For every football they sell, a football goes to a deprived child; now they have to send thousands of footballs to children in over 40 countries. In 2008 on a trip to Honduras, the founders were asked to help the local community to sell their coffee, thereby helping the families to a sustainable income. Stefan didn't need to think long and now there is Little Feet coffee, all adding to more footballs for children to play with.

So what is it your business can do, what can you add? What makes you and your business unique? Tom's Shoes started on the simple promise that for every pair of Tom's shoes purchased they would give a pair to a child in need. Millions of people in the world have no shoes to wear. Tom saw this on a trip a few years ago and decided he could do something about it. Being barefoot can cause many diseases and cuts and bruises; many children can't attend school because shoes are an integral part of the school uniform and they are not allowed to enter school without shoes. Tom is a true social entrepreneur.

There are many great examples; however, when you choose the cause you support or the type of business you set up, be careful that what you do connects exactly with your customers and what they want. It can backfire. A good example is Airtran – a budget airline which recently announced that they are selling the world's first carbon-neutral water, Icelandic Glacial water, and it is served in PET bottles. Icelandic water all the way to New Zealand? Bottled water gets banned in more and more places. Does using an eco-friendly bottle and buying carbon offsets discount the fact that the water is travelling thousands of miles? Why not do as I have seen on Virgin flights: a water cooler in the middle of the plane with a cup dispenser. That is thinking about all angles of our challenges.

A London advertising company had the idea to offer companies advertising on water bottles which would be given for free to the travelling public on hot days. The idea behind it is that the consumer appreciates getting something for free at a time he really appreciates it and he keeps the bottle with him for some time, giving you ample opportunity to do some great branding. A good idea at first sight; however, it is bottled water. What if we spent some time coming up with an even more innovative and green solution? How about placing water coolers available for the public with sustainable cups, or hand out tap water with a campaign stating why your company supports that initiative? It needs careful thinking when you design your strategies.

Water is an interesting subject. Wars will be fought in the future over our water resources. Ldesh Fresh is an unusual take on the bottled water campaign, branded as the world's water, introducing the world's most authentic drinking water. It shows you how good we have it in the developed world, to have so much choice. We have water on tap or in a bottle, while the quality most people on this planet use is just appalling. Ldesh Fresh shows you in bottles the water that two billion people in the world have to drink as they have no access to clean water. The smelly dirty water is, therefore, the biggest water 'brand' in the world. Ldesh Fresh tries to get us to take action by shocking us.
The bottom billion can definitely use help in the branding of their products in order to compete with our large companies and to find the right markets. Good branding can help many small entrepreneurs in developing countries.

Neal and Amy Carter have set up Guludo lodges in Mozambique. Together they had a dream: their idea was to create an innovative and sustainable model to relieve poverty and protect the environment. The result was

Guludo Beach Lodge and its associated charity, Nema Foundation. Donating 5% of its income to the charity, the lodge maximises the benefits to the local area whilst the charity, Nema Foundation, implements a wide array of community and conservation projects. Although in its infancy, this model has since become an award-winning and internationally-applauded strategy for addressing extreme rural poverty and environmental degradation. I have met Amy and she is wonderful – having a dream and going after it 100%. She showed us how they worked together with the local people to produce everything for the lodges, using local materials. The only thing imported was the scuba-diving equipment. The foundation now supports hundreds of children in the local school.

Jamie Oliver did a great job when he set up Fifteen restaurant in London, training 15 homeless unemployed young people at a time. A very commendable and successful effort which now has many followers, and many restaurants around the globe are following the same concept. Jamie set it up because he wanted to give young people a chance in an industry which gave him so much. It is a great concept which not only trains many disadvantaged young people, it is also a commercial success. Think about what you can do. How can you use your skills to train or educate young people? Education, training and skills are very important tools to use to help others to achieve their dreams. It is also very fulfilling for yourself if you help somebody to get mastery in what they do. I believe that the understanding of achieving mastery in a subject or profession helps you in everything else you do and that things become easier. The confidence knowing that you have done it once helps you to achieve it with every new goal you set yourself.

CSR policies from large companies are often paying lip service, or it is used as a clever marketing tool, employing clever copywriters. If you dig a little deeper, you will see that many companies don't actually do an awful lot. Just recently, I was given the UK guide to company giving; it reviews FTSE 500 companies and what they give back to the community. Profit margins range from tens of millions to billions and the average percentage of giving back makes you want to cry. It is a lot less than the general public give; the average company gives 0.6% of their net profit. That number is very disappointing; imagine what good causes and companies could do together when they align with each other.

When you start to look around, there are great causes you can align your business with. Whenever I am doing research, I am amazed about the great causes and not-for-profits that people have set up. I am 100% sure the right cause/project is there for you with which to establish a great partnership – causes like the Smile Foundation which helps children with a cleft palate. In India, 35,000 children every year are born with a cleft palate and they become social outcasts, facing shame and isolation; there are literally hundreds of thousands of cases. Smile Foundation helps with corrective surgery, transforming tens of thousands of lives. A great cause for a coach or personal development company; what empowerment would that be?

Social entrepreneurship in the developing world

Social enterprise is also a beautiful way in the developing world to do something about the challenges we face. We can do that in two ways. Businesses in the western world can help and support solutions to save our planet, help the poor and support the Millennium Development Goals. The other way is via social enterprises which are set up by people in the developing world. Entrepreneurs change the world; governments rarely do, with some exceptions – for example, in Belo Horizonte. Poverty makes people very entrepreneurial and innovative. We must support the bottom billion by giving them the tools to help themselves out of poverty. We can do this by empowerment, asking them what they need and what they want. The Hunger Project does this through giving visioning workshops for women, giving courses, microfinance and building epicentres which help a whole area out of hunger.

Microfinance has created millions of opportunities for people to start a business or sometimes to buy a cow or goat to feed their family. Out of small microloans, the most amazing projects have started. An estimated 2.5 billion people in the world have no access to basic sanitation. Entrepreneur David Kuria decided to do something about it and he set up a 'toilet mall' in Kibera, Nairobi. His company Ecotact builds toilet malls, creates demand and supplies the maintenance. "Why just do two quick things in the toilet?" Kuria asks. Ecotact builds toilet malls that provide bathroom facilities along with shoe shines, food, phone booths and other commercial services. Each toilet complex is equipped with eight toilets, a water kiosk, a baby-changing station and gender-separate showers; 30,000 customers use Ecotact's facilities every day. Other business opportunities are now coming his way as he gets offers to put advertisements in the malls and local vendors are keen to keep the toilets clean in order for them also to attract more business. It is the business model that drives his success, although it started by doing good. This is a model which can be replicated easily. Users pay a few cents for a basic need they don't have in their homes. Providing water and sanitation is also a great business model, averaging about $9 for every dollar invested.

Harish Hande set up Selco Solar in 1995. Selco sells $100 solar lighting systems to the poor. He has convinced microfinance institutions to help people to buy the installations as it is beneficial to their life and education. He has now sold over 10,000 solar panels in Kundapura, 'town of the sun.' Aiming to sell more than 200,000 systems in the next four years, Harish's social enterprise is determined to illuminate the poorest of the poor areas in the country. He started with many people telling him it couldn't be done and would be too expensive. After a slow start, he got more and more support. A few of Selco's first customers have made their own businesses from the solar panels they installed. I have read stories of people who offer locals the chance to charge their batteries on the solar panels they have installed, thereby helping their neighbours who haven't been able to afford the panels yet. Harish is a true social entrepreneur; he saw a problem and decided to do something about it, letting nothing stop him. He is creating a ripple effect and, under the lights which can be run because of the solar panels, many children and adults can now study in the evening. A fact we often overlook is that in rural India electricity is often rare, very unreliable or only available a few hours per day.

I love the stories, large and small, from entrepreneurs in the developing world, hearing the adversity they had to overcome to start their business and get it going. The strength and determination they show puts most of us to shame. If we could have the same energy, strength and courage for our businesses or jobs, I believe the results we would achieve would be a lot greater. In India we met a barber who had set up shop under a tree, weather permitting, but his customers knew they could find him there.

"In a world where change is escalating exponentially, the only way we'll make it is if everyone has the mindset of a social entrepreneur."

Bill Drayton

When you travel around the world to any tourist site you usually find hundreds of salesmen trying to sell you handicrafts, souvenirs or photographs. They are often very much in your face. When you live a life of poverty, you will do anything to provide for your family and you'll see every tourist as an opportunity. Many tourists are opposed to the salesmen but I admire their determination. How often have you been photographed, declined to buy the photo and hours later they found you miles further, still trying to sell you their photos? Most of us would have long given up, wouldn't we? OK, maybe it would be best to find products or services the tourists really want, or don't sell them the same as all the others do. However, I believe we can learn as much from them as they can learn from us.

Argan trees are only found in the south-west of Morocco. They are made famous by the goats that climb the trees to eat the nuts; when you visit Morocco it is a must-see sight. The nuts make the most beautiful oil, soap and beauty products but it is a very time-consuming job crushing the nuts to extract the oil, which can only be done by hand. In recent years, the products have become very sought-after by restaurants and shops. Now some cooperatives are set up by women. Collectively they own the cooperative and share the workload, focusing on each other's strengths and using marketing and the internet to sell the products abroad. All the women employed are divorced from their husbands and have no other means of income; working times are organised around school times and even child care is shared. The women have become independent, are proud of what they are doing and are helping their surroundings with the money they earn. Groups of women working together are an important part of the microfinance strategy all over the world. Women in general care more for their larger family and immediate surroundings than men.

What can you do in your business?

Everyone has the opportunity to do something in their business. I remember when we were on our trip to India standing in the fields thinking there was nothing I could do with my skills. It was just a matter of perception; I realised that there were many things I could do.

Cameron Stewart in Ireland has set up a not-for-profit clothing brand called Act of Random Kindness. The idea is that every time you wear one of their items of clothing or other products, you perform a random act of kindness. The idea comes from the fact that we are all thinking about ourselves and what if we could all be a bit kinder to each other. Oneness can go a long way. This is what they say on their own website: we'd like to promote something a bit more meaningful, a society where people of all ages take some time out and do something thoughtful for someone else on a regular basis. Just share a moment before moving on with the same journey. It's not going to change the world but if enough people do it, it can slowly usher in a society of better people that's nicer to live in – a society that sees the importance of I because of the strength of We. Cameron and his friends were teenagers when they started ARK, an initiative to be applauded and supported.

Yvon Chouinard is founder of outdoor clothing and gear company Patagonia. His first success was as a rock climber. He recognised early on that the financial success of the company provided the ideal opportunity to also achieve personal goals. Chouinard committed the company to being an outstanding place to work and an important resource for environmental activism. Some of the early initiatives Patagonia undertook were on-site cafeterias offering healthy, mostly vegetarian food and on-site child care. In 1986, the company started 'tithing' for environmental activism, committing 1% of sales or 10% of profits, whichever was the greater. Clean climbing was pioneered and, in the early 1990s, the company committed to using all pesticide-free (i.e. organically-grown) cotton. This demand created the organic cotton industry in California.

Patagonia is now one of the best examples of how we can do business in a different way. Yvon has published works on green marketing and other subjects. Just recently, I read an article on how their turnover went up in an effort to reduce packaging. Yvon wanted to get rid of packaging on underwear; everybody advised him against it as they believed consumers wouldn't accept it, but it became a huge success with growing sales figures.

"People of character do right the thing not because they think it'll change the world but because they refuse to be changed by the world."

M. Josephson

When you are looking at what you can do in your business, always make sure you keep it simple. Start with just one thing. The idea has to fit on the back of a business card – or the back of a beer mat, as they say in England. Discuss your idea with a few friends in a pub and make your idea so simple it fits on the back of a beer mat. If you can't do it, make it simpler. Patagonia started with a simple idea and then built on that. We entrepreneurs often feel we can do everything, add everything to our business, we jump at every opportunity. But if you find that one thing you are No. 1 at, you can build a huge business just within your field of expertise. Roger Hamilton says that, very often, you grow by what you say no to. Last year, when I was doing my research for Extraordinary Ones, I thought we could do our concept on everything: food, T-shirts, coaching, corporate. You name it and I would be creative. As a result, people were lost after talking to somebody like me, they weren't sure any more what we stood for. And it was right; in my head it was clear, I was eager to start but wasn't really getting anywhere. As soon as we narrowed down our concept – for every meal you buy you feed a child – everything became very clear and people showed up, wanted to help and take part and, more importantly, we could explain it in ten seconds flat. It had become the ideal elevator pitch. I realised by doing just that one thing we could become really big, have huge impact and make a real difference.

The advice I have been given by several mentors in my past boils down to the following:

- start small

- think big

- be smart

- act fast

I really love short, bold and quick steps. Just as we did for Extraordinary Ones, all the time three benchmarks:

- scalable

- huge impact

- everyone has to be able to take part

Keep this in mind after you have found your purpose and add that to your business. Start small. Wal-Mart started as a small grocery shop and grew very quickly to the largest supermarket chain in the world. Wal-Mart listens to its customers really well; now it has a very progressive CSR policy supporting change and sustainability. 'Be smart' for me tells you a lot about the way you run your business. All the time focus on what is the best way of doing things, focus on your core business and what adds value to your mission and vision. When it doesn't, you shouldn't be do-ing it; outsource it and let specialists do it, work together with companies who are better at supplying that particular service. Be smart and look at which partnerships you can set up in order to grow your business. Remember, in this age it is all about working together and being one.

Chapter 9 Business making a difference

Chapter 10

The solutions are already there

Entrepreneurs change the world. Everyone can be an entrepreneur and that revolution is already with us. People under 30 nowadays are not expected to work in the same job for more than three years on average. The rise of companies and websites helping you to set up your own business, business schools, tools or getting a mentor is truly staggering and really exciting. I see new developments all the time; probably the most popular competitions at the moment are the ones where you can send in your idea and either judges or the public decide which one is the best. Even on the TV, you have shows like *Dragon's Den* becoming ever more popular, the Dragons have become stars – something which simply wouldn't have happened 10-15 years ago. The best idea receives funding, mentoring or resources. This is a revolution I am very passionate about and believe it is a great way forward. In 2020 most of us will be small entrepreneurs or, at the very least, self-employed, specialising all in our own little niche and, of course, contributing to our own purpose. Imagine what the world would look like then, everybody doing what they love best and having fun doing it.

The resources we have available in this age make it possible to do this. We work the hours we want in our virtual offices. The internet makes it possible to store your documents securely online and you can access them anywhere. You can take payments anywhere, any time and mobile technology has made that even easier; there are applications which take credit card payment on the spot.

Nothing in this respect stops you from starting whatever you want, even resources. Whatever you need to start your project, there is a way of getting what you need. What do you believe is holding you back? Can everything be achieved in other ways, through collaboration with like-minded individuals who have the right skills set or tools you need to achieve your goal? Start talking about your idea, share it with as many people as possible and let them know what you are looking for. At the same time, keep building on your idea. Who remembers the movie *Field of Dreams* with Kevin Costner as a farmer who has a dream to build a baseball pitch on his farm? He starts to build the pitch against much adversity and through difficult financial times on his farm. He 'hears' voices which tell him, 'build it and they'll come' and 'go the distance.' Right in the middle of a cornfield, he builds the field with bleachers and floodlights.

His wife is semi-supportive but is worried about their finances. No-one but those who believe can see the ghostly ballplayers who begin to appear. At the end of the movie, when his wife tells him not to sell the farm, all of a sudden many people turn up. They show up because they believe and can also see the players. This is a great story of how life unfolds right in front of our eyes. When you have a purpose that is bigger than yourself, there is nothing stopping you. Always keep going, especially when times are tough. When you build it the right way, people to support you will show up; it may be customers, donors, investors, I promise you they will show up. Kevin's character believed in his vision and that is why he saw the players and, as soon as others started to believe as well, they could also see the players.

For all the challenges we face in our time we have the solutions as well. We have to become one, connected from within our hearts and see what we really need to do on our planet. Lynn Twist talks about sufficiency on the global sufficiency network:

'Sufficiency is the radical surprising truth about life. Sufficiency is the state of being, the state of knowing, the state of relating to the world that there is enough. And when you lift the veil of scarcity, when you get out of the chase for more and actually pay attention to what's already there, you start to see that life meets you exactly where you are and gives you exactly what you need. It's not an amount of anything. It's a way of being, a way of seeing, a way of living.

In fact, there is a principle of sufficiency that I believe really says it all, and that is: If you let go of trying to get more of what you don't really need, it frees up oceans of energy to pay attention to, and make a difference with, what you already have. When you make a difference with what you have, it expands. Another way of saying this is: what you appreciate appreciates. So, when we pay attention to what we have, when we let go of trying to get more, we can live in a state of being where we see that there's enough.'

Evolution

So how did we get here? What happened that we arrived at this point of disruption? For millions of years, the planet evolved slowly, the evolution took care of everything and our beautiful planet evolved to what it is now. As we as people evolved, we started to feel superior and believed we were above nature and other species. At first we lived in villages together, one with each other and our surroundings. Slowly we started to claim land and resources, taking more than we needed, using wood or oil from the Earth which are not really resources to use. When you are hungry tonight you will not cut up your arm or burn the leg of your table just because you are cold. These are not resources. As humanity developed faster, we started to live in a dream and thought we needed more and more to satisfy our ever-growing need. In the last century, we grew from two to six billion inhabitants. We wanted ever-bigger cars, larger houses, better machines, larger fridges and garages full of stuff, the dream being that wanting and needing ever more would satisfy us. In the meantime, we have lost our connections with each other, the people around us, the ones who really matter. As a result, we use ever more resources of our planet, doing increasingly more damage, justifying it because we 'need' it. But do we need more stuff? We are stealing from the planet at such a rate that evolution cannot keep up any more. Earth is such a wonderful mechanism that evolution has managed to deal with everything: ice ages, huge meteors or diseases spreading over continents. However, the speed at which we are destroying things now is of such a pace that Earth can't keep up any more. Urgent action is required or we face extinction.

It is not just the speed of destruction that has been increasing; in the last 50 years, life has started to speed up. It took 30 years after the first telephone call before telephones started to be taken seriously. The internet is really only 15 years old and has close to two billion users. The first company to reach a billion dollar valuation did that in 80 years; Facebook needed just two years to do it.

The speed at which things are happening has put us in this state; the beauty is that the same speed will help us out of it. There is a huge movement coming forward, a movement of millions of individuals and organisations, a civil movement. People like you and me who know what their calling is and what they can do. All of us coming together playing our role will make sure that the evolution keeps going. This movement of people is so strong that nothing can stop it. Millions of people who follow their higher purpose, knowing that nothing can stop us. When you meet somebody who has found their higher purpose, you know, you can see it in their eyes and feel it in their actions. These are the people who you trust immediately and you know they go out and do things and achieve what they set out to do. All of us together will change the planet and make us come together. Are you part of us, that civil movement?

What is the Vision?

The solutions for whatever we have faced – be it on this planet in your business or in your life – have always been within us. Our collective knowledge or infinite wisdom has the solutions and they come to us often in the most unexpected ways. Book printing was invented in two totally different places at the same time; penicillin was discovered at the right time. These inventions come from our collective wisdom and show up at the right time, we have the solutions amongst us at any time. The same goes for the challenges we have in our time; we need to apply our collective wisdom to let the solutions come out. Will we pass our final exam, as Buckminster Fuller would say? On a personal level, this goes as well; you have never been given a dream or solution without the resources you need to make your dream come true or solve your challenges. Whatever you need is already in your network, look within yourself and you get the answers you need.

Many great discoveries, insights or answers come to us via visionaries such as Buckminster Fuller, Muhammed Yunus, Jacqueline Novogratz of Acumen Fund or Jacque Fresco of the Venus project. We need the insights of these brilliant people to push the boundaries, explore opportunities, push us further to be bold, brave and keep us moving forward at speed.

Let us talk about some of the solutions we have within us, solutions which don't drain our resources but bank on the abundance or sufficiency we have in our eco system. By tapping into this we will move forward without draining our resources. We will be able to leave a positive net impact on the planet and the people living on it.

This is not meant to be an extensive list, just a few examples I have picked up on. Space solar energy: I know of a few companies who are working on this. You can imagine that we can build huge solar panels which float around in space, no clouds or Earth movement which can stop them getting radiation from the sun. Solar energy in this way is a very interesting, clean and sustainable energy solution. The technology to get the energy to Earth via radio waves is built and a great option. It will mean huge up-front investment but it will be a reality very soon. Wind energy is not seen by experts as a large-scale solution; it works perfectly well on a smaller scale and together with other energy sources. Tidal wave energy which can be extracted just by the movement of the sea in huge 'fins'. The currents of the sea never stop; it is a clean, reliable and sustainable source of energy. Another opportunity is using the heat in the Earth as a source of energy. At the current usage levels we have, there is enough to supply the needs of the whole planet for 3,000 years. There are enough options to clean energy to stop us using oil, coal or biodiesel.

Our forests have been dwindling; in the last 60 years we lost 60% of our rainforest. Reforestation helps to reduce poverty, provides sustainable food production, regulates water and controls climate change. Losing our forests has caused many problems like erosion, degrading of our land, pollution and loss of cloud cover which adds to global warming and, therefore, affects the environment. Did you know that an acre of permadesign food forest could sustainably support 10 people, an acre of wheat only five people and we need oil to help in the production? Permaculture is an approach to designing human settlements and agriculture systems that mimics the relationships found in natural ecologies. Permaculture is definitely a solution we have to develop. Join the schemes which are there, plant trees in your area or help to build forests. A good example is what Willie Smits is doing in Indonesia. Living there, he has set up a reserve to save orang-utans. He found out about the sugar palm. In Asia, three plants are the basis of everything they do and they are the basis of life: banana, palm and bamboo. Each of them can be used in multiple sustainable ways for food, building, tools or clothes and many other things. The beauty is that when you cut off a bamboo shoot it keeps growing; from a banana tree you can keep using the leaves or bark and you don't damage the tree, it just keeps growing.

Willie discovered that you can tap the sugar of the sugar palm just like we do with a rubber tree. He calls the sugar palm a magic tree as everything can be used and it is actually good for humans from the root to the leaf. It is also very good in fighting erosion because of its roots. The extract is traditionally used to make sugar or alcohol. Willie discovered it can be made into ethanol – alternative fuel. The tree doesn't have to be cut down and you can keep making ethanol out of it. Small refineries have been built which fit on the back of a small lorry so locals can produce their own fuel from their own sugar palms. With three sugar palms you can earn about $6 a day working less than two hours or use it as your own energy source. More importantly, it is a never-ending source of energy growing in your backyard. This is real permaculture, especially if you have other plants and trees growing around it supplying food. Growing our food more locally is part of our future. Willie's project is making a huge difference for thousands of Indonesians who can now use some of the resources they have available already. They can produce the ethanol locally, sell it and run their machines on it – starting new businesses, for example. Willie is now looking to take his project to many places all over the world. Sustainable sugar palm is a great local solution and palm is a very versatile crop which can be used in many ways. Palm oil, however, is not a solution and is a problem causing many of acres of rainforest to be cut.

Detroit, the city which was once everything America stood for, all the large car manufacturers were based there, has seen an enormous decline for decades now. Many buildings are empty and there are whole areas in the city where hardly anyone wants to live. It looked almost like the lost city and it is hard to believe it once played such an important role. In this state of destruction, others who are looking for freedom are now flocking to Detroit. Now Detroit is a city of Hope rather than a city of Despair. The thousands of vacant lots and abandoned houses not only provide the space to begin again but also the incentive to create innovative ways of making a living – ways that nurture our productive, cooperative and caring selves. A quiet revolution is taking place; the community is coming together and is creating a new economy. Gardens are sprouting up everywhere, run by the community, helping to fight rising food prices but, more importantly, global warming. The people of Detroit are coming together, creating self-esteem, healthy food, leadership skills, a base for economic development, a sense of belonging and connectedness. It shows that when necessity drives us we do find the solutions and we come together. It took Detroit right until the end; a city which used to be run by the police and military has turned a corner and is now an example for others. Again, this is a trend we should see worldwide: community gardens, urban gardens on greens, roofs and open spaces to grow more of our own local food. It is possible to grow enough food for a family of four all year round on three square metres, suitable for almost every garden. I know of a design of a one square metre pyramid which, carefully designed and planted, will have the same results, climate permitting, but should suit many people in, for example, Australia, southern Europe and the south of the US.

Jacque Fresco's work on the Venus project is less well-known than Buckminster Fuller; he is a visionary and ahead of his time. Jacques believes that in order to keep world peace we have to redesign the way we live. We have to move beyond a money-based economy. His vision is to move to a resource-based economy where there is no money, everybody cooperates and where we eliminate boring tasks which are replaced by machines powered by clean and efficient energy. Jacque envisions a high standard of living and abundance for everyone if we start giving up money totally. In the movie *The Zeitgeist Movement* you see his view of how money has corrupted our thinking and our systems. Although we will need to move to an in-between state, a money-free society is a dream which is worth fostering. In recent years, we have seen the rise of bartering and local currencies which is a nice trend, trying to empower local economies and say no to the force of some global institutions.

There are many more examples of solutions for our challenges. Start to follow a few people's blogs, talk to others, look on the websites of the people I have mentioned and you will find a world opening up to this movement which is really inspiring, mind-blowing and will give you many ideas.

Changing your business

Could any of the ideas inspire you to change your business or be the spark for a new idea?

Acumen Fund is a non-profit global venture fund that uses entrepreneurial approaches to solve the problems of global poverty. Jacqueline Novogratz who founded Acumen realised that the poor are very often not interesting for the financial market. Great solutions need philanthropic capital and some business acumen to help them grow and deliver real affordable solutions for people in developing countries. Focused on affordable, critical goods and services like water, health and energy that serve vast amounts of people, Jacqueline has backed projects like Vision-Spring. VisionSpring supplies affordable spectacles costing between $2.5 and $4. Over 400 million people across the developing world suffer from presbyopia – deterioration of the eyes that comes with middle-age – and they have no access to affordable spectacles. Spectacles often mean the difference between income or not. The VisionSpring model is via microfranchise to train many Vision entrepreneurs, empowering thousands of people, securing them an income. The model works in two ways: ensuring the franchise holders an income and helping the people to whom they supply spectacles. VisionSpring was the vision of one man who has tapped into a demand which was overlooked by companies supplying the West as they believed the market was not interesting.

Another example is Husk Power Systems. In rural India for example, 56% of households have no electricity; especially in the rice-growing states, the percentage of villages with no electricity is 90%. Husk Power Systems (HPS) uses novel biomass technology to convert rice husks into combustible gases. The gases drive a generator to produce clean, safe and efficient electricity. These rice husks have no economic value and have previously been left to rot in fields, releasing harmful methane into the atmosphere. It not only supplies the people with clean energy from a material which was not used before, it also creates jobs at the plant and helps businesses.

An entrepreneur from Norway came up with a great idea: a stove made out of two cardboard boxes. Rather than sending the boxes to landfill, the cardboard stove, called the Kyoto Box, has been designed for developing countries – for less than $5. The box is aimed at people living in rural areas, now mainly using kerosene or firewood. This takes them hours to collect and, in the process of cutting down trees, they harm the climate and their own surroundings, as we know how harmful the cutting of trees is. Through a transparent acrylic lid, the air is trapped and it is enough to boil water or fry food. The stove can halve the use of firewood or poisonous fuels like kerosene which damage the health of the users. Kyoto's Energy Box is now in production and they hope to reach 500 million people. I like the idea and brilliance of what they have done: using what is already there to provide a solution. As with every idea, they have to come up with sustainable solutions on the impact of transport of the boxes. It does, however, make us think outside the box and look at what we have already.

My friend Phyllis has been working in microfinance for a long time; she loves the concept and is passionate in helping it grow. She also saw that some issues needed addressing in order to push it to the next level. Many people get a microloan but unfortunately have no basic understanding of money management or business. There are far too few trainers to look after the people who get loans as they are over-stretched. Phyllis has set up a new business called Microfinance Without Borders. The main thing they do is to train people in the West to go and help trainers in the field. This way, the borrowers (entrepreneurs) get supported better, have a higher success rate and you empower more people to come out of poverty. MWB gives courses mainly to students, financial institutions and anyone who likes to spend some time in the field, helping and empowering budding entrepreneurs.

'Poor' is a word I don't like to use; when you call people 'poor' you put them in a box which is not very empowering. Some people are resource-poor and this might have happened because they have been left out of the systems for years or generations. Often whole families, areas or whole countries are left behind at the same time. When you are right at the bottom, you need a helping hand or lift to get out of your situation. A **hand up**, not a **hand-out**. What we call poor people are often some of the strongest and finest people you can find. They are more whole than we are; because of their situation, they are more connected to each other and understand the true meaning of life. They see the beauty in the little things. I feel we have to find a different word for people who are resource-poor; any ideas? 'Poor' puts you in a certain place, I am sure that is not what we are meant to do; often these people are a lot stronger than us and are not chasing our dream of 'ever more'. Because we are all one, what should it be?

What would you do if you had nothing? What would you do if you woke up tomorrow and everything you have wouldn't be worth anything? Your house, your savings and shares, how would that make you feel? Many people would feel relieved; no more job to go to that they hate, not worrying about the mortgage to pay or the bigger car they 'need'. How would you feel? What would you do? Imagine if all of us were resource-poor; I am sure the first thing we would to do is connect with each other, there would be more real conversations between us all again. We would start to care more for each other rather than just looking for what we can get. We would be free and the circumstances would push us to work out the solutions. In reality, what is happening in Detroit of all places!

In London in 2000, Carmel McConnell came across a shocking report. The report stated that, for one in four UK schoolchildren, the only hot meal they receive each day is at school. Their hunger left them feeling upset, tired and irritable, unable to settle or concentrate on their lessons. Their behaviour is difficult and, because of their hunger and low concentration, study results are poor.

Carmel started delivering breakfasts to six schools in Hackney; now she delivers breakfasts to over 3,000 children every day. Carmel has set up a social enterprise to fund her cause. Magic Outcomes is an innovative social enterprise which provides schools with training, and development programmes to organisations which seek to pursue their commercial objectives alongside socially responsible outcomes. A cool business which empowers schools and uses the proceeds to fund her cause of feeding children. An excellent example of how a business can have a huge impact.

Don't forget to have fun whilst doing it

If you love what you do and it is connected to your purpose, you have a rock-solid combination. Make sure you have fun while doing it; first of all, it makes everything you do so much easier, your results will be better and people will want to work with you. Make sure when you plan what you want to do, when you plan how your business is going to make a difference, that you have the fun element in it as well; there is always a way. Fun stands for creating it in the most pleasurable way for yourself and others. A few years ago, I decided that I wanted to work from home more and I wanted to travel more, see great places and meet people from all over the world. Travel is definitely one of the things I enjoy doing most. When I decided to work more from home, we still had our wholesale business which was very time-consuming and labour-intensive. That was the way I created it. Six months later, when I was walking the children to school one morning, I realised that I had achieved one of my goals and I didn't realise it. I had been working from home for four months by that time, having most meals together now with my family. No way would I ever go back.

Make sure you do what you do best. I am very good at coming up with new concepts and starting them out of nothing, creating the opportunities. I also see intuitively in which direction others need to go. I love doing that for many hours and that is how I came up with the concept of Extraordinary Ones. Extraordinary Ones is my purpose of being here, ending world hunger. Following that through is giving me many new opportunities. I decided a while ago that I would focus only on what I am best at, enjoy doing and how I could make the biggest difference. What you appreciate appreciates – that always works. Sure, there have been challenges but when you have a higher vision you always have to keep going, particularly when it gets tough. Have your eye on the goal and keep going; if it is your purpose, nothing can stop you.

For a while, I was involved in a business that sold food in boxes on subscription. We decided that not only the products we sold should be sustainable and of the highest quality, but also the packaging should be just that. We sourced beautiful banana leaf boxes from Asia; remember, a sustainable material. We helped the local community there by supporting local businesses and the company had an edge because of the beautiful packaging. Customers kept the boxes and used them for all sorts of reasons; the boxes were used as gifts. It was definitely fun designing and creating all that.

The town of Budanoon in Australia decided to become the first town to ban bottled water. The residents were motivated by environmental campaigns and created a social movement within the city. To keep people hydrated, local businesses now refill water bottles for free and the city plans to install public water fountains throughout the town. Bundanoon's ban will reduce plastic waste, mobilise the city to develop its public water resources and, most importantly, spark communities around the world to follow suit. I think it is a fun campaign and does lots of good. If you could go in anywhere to ask to fill up your water bottle, that is very cool and creates community spirit.

Pepsi recently launched Pepsi Refresh. It is giving away a huge part of the money it would normally spend on advertising during the Superbowl final. The way it works is that they are looking for people, businesses, and not-for-profit organisations with ideas that will have a positive impact. When you have an idea, you can submit it and apply for funding and the public will vote every month for the best ideas. Your idea can get up to $250,000. Pepsi has developed a fun way of spending advertising money in a different way, motivating people to do good, and it gives them a lot of great publicity at the same time. I believe this is a great idea which we need to applaud; more corporations should follow. You can use these kinds of ideas for your own business. How can you interact with your customers, motivate them to do good, and create positive PR?

Similar initiatives have started all over the world – campaigns to stop using plastic bags, for example. What is fun is different for all of us but it is up to you to include it in your business, the way you make yours work or how you make a difference. It can be in little things; young people nowadays live on Facebook and are on it all the time. I think Twitter is fun as I can follow the most inspiring and amazing people, but others don't see always the point. Smart phone applications don't just add convenience, they can also add a lot of fun. You see, it is up to you, it is all there. How do you create fun in your business?

Chhapter 10 The solutions are already there

Chapter 11

Transformational giving

The value of giving back, or donating, by normal people like you and me is very often undervalued. When big corporations give a large amount of money to a charity or a good cause, it is news because of the big amount and the clever PR machines they employ to highlight their gifts. When rich people give a substantial amount of their money, the same happens. Many people then feel left out; what difference can I make? My donation is not significant. There are two factors to this: firstly, corporate giving is only between 8-10% of giving in total and philanthropy, however generous, as we call the second is about 7% of giving back. At best, together they are no more than 15-18% of giving back in total annually. So all the other donations (over 80%) come from small donations, from people like you and me.

Did you know that philanthropy means the love of human kind? It has nothing to do with the amount you give; the reasons why you give are the most important. Make sure it comes from your heart. Give because you really want to. Don't give just because you can, but give in a way that resonates with you 100% and the more effective your giving back is for you. You are a philanthropist.

Often, large companies give an amount of money to a certain cause one year and the next year they look to give it to another cause. Although well intended, this is not very sustainable for the causes, as the following year they have to look where they can find a similar amount of money, thereby spending much time and resources on fundraising, which is not necessarily their strength. A good thing which is happening is that businesses are increasingly searching for partnerships with causes, building long-term relationships. For a cause, just like a business, the money flow which you have coming in on a regular basis is the most important, creating a platform on which to build and expand. Cause marketing and transactional giving do just that!

What is transactional giving?

Transactional giving is where every transaction adds to more, not less. Every transaction creates positive change, every dollar you spend goes to both consumption for yourself and contributions to others. Every transaction makes a difference in the lives of others. It will transform the world by the choices you make. We will become more conscious consumers, every purchase we make will make the connections between us as humankind stronger. That creates positive change through exchange. Then transactional will become transformational.

There are three words which come back all the time in my opinion: give, share and connect. Every time you buy something for yourself, you share something with someone who is not as fortunate as you. It helps us to come out of our dream of 'not enough' to realise we have abundance. Basically, it is about amounts so small it doesn't make a difference to you but, added up, will transform the lives of others.

Extraordinary Ones is transactional giving; every time you buy a meal, 20 pence goes towards helping others who are hungry.

It is very powerful to connect to a good scheme or to set one up in your own business. Customers want you to. Transactional giving is a form of cause marketing at its best. Whatever you choose, make sure that the giving back goes on every product a customer buys or as part of the end bill. Often you see that companies have transactional giving just on one product that they are offering; this means that when you don't buy that particular product as a customer, you are not contributing. Giving back or transformational giving should run through your whole business, not as a small part of it. When we all do this, giving back becomes even stronger. Imagine you run a café and, for every meal you sell, 20 pence goes towards feeding other people. You can also sell a fruit juice which donates a small amount per bottle sold to water projects in Africa. The giving back just keeps doubling up. But be aware that the scheme you offer is genuine and offers real advantages to giving back. For example, many supermarkets have set up similar schemes which seem very generous but are often just a way to lure in more customers. Generous as they seem at first, free school equipment vouchers are just a clever strategy where the gift back is actually very low.

At some of the big supermarkets, you receive one voucher for every £10 you spend at the stores. So if your local school wants a new computer (let's say, an Apple iMac), it would first have to collect 25,640 vouchers – or spend more than a quarter of a million pounds at the store. It's no easier to earn a 'free' printer. For a basic model, you'd need to spend more than £40,000 in store (that's 4,040 vouchers); for 12 children's basketball bibs, you'll need to run up a £29,500 grocery bill; and for a free book about birds, you'll have to spend £6,300, which is especially ludicrous as the book only costs £6.99 in the first place. As customers become more informed and 'enlightened', I believe these schemes will work against the companies who deploy them.

How have I built Extraordinary Ones?

"Imagine all the people, sharing all the world. You may say I'm a dreamer, but I'm not the only one, I hope someday you'll join us, and the world will live as one."

John Lennon

In earlier chapters, I explained to you what my motivation was to set up Extraordinary Ones. Let me explain to you how we have built it. I started with a few key words, setting up a business whose sole purpose is to help end world hunger. I have been lucky to have had a few great mentors in the last few years and their advice has helped me enormously. Always make sure you have smarter people than yourself around you to help and advise you. We came up with three key goals for Extraordinary Ones:

- it had to be able to deliver huge impact

- everybody had to be able to take part

- it had to be totally scalable

The first idea was to start selling food boxes which would feed children at the same time. This required a lot of manpower, stock and distribution challenges so it didn't deliver on any of our objectives. A great idea, nonetheless, which we might develop later with a specialist company. Once we started talking to food producers about this idea, they all got very excited and wanted to become part of what we did. The idea of the concept started to move more towards certification. This meant that when you saw our logo you would know that the product would be part of our standard. The certification would show that a certain amount was given to charity; it would be a similar thing to organic or fair-trade labels. This idea was already more scalable and, therefore, could have a huge impact. The difficulties with certification are that you need to govern it, have rules and regulations. These are all bottlenecks. Who checks or polices your policy, who decides what is right or wrong? It was becoming very impractical and who would pay for it? The way to grow your business and make it huge is by constantly removing all bottlenecks. The beauty of the internet and the resources we have available nowadays means that this is possible. We thought about asking businesses for a percentage of their turnover or profit and giving them gold, silver and bronze logos depending on the percentage, making it more complicated to communicate, involving more costs, and even more difficult to immediately understand and less interesting to take part. All the time I was thinking about this, I had a vision of seeing our logo all over restaurants, menus, windows and on lots of products in shops. "What does a percentage of profit mean anyway?" you might say, "I give 10% of my profit but you hardly make any profit or does the public understand how much 10% is, what does it mean?" The danger with that idea was also that large businesses could get our certification at a very low cost to them but they would be connected to making a difference. The danger was it made the businesses look good but without necessarily doing that much good. Exactly what I don't like in many CSR policies, it could be just a PR exercise. So we stopped with this idea.

Because of our research, we knew that it costs 25 cents a day to feed a child or $91.25 for a whole year. The next idea was easily found: every donation of $100 would feed a child for a year and cover a little of the overheads of Extraordinary Ones. A business would decide how many children it wants to help every year. For $1,000 they help 10 children; for $10,000 the number is 100. The business would get our logo with the number of children they feed underneath. So by buying from the company, you knew exactly how many children you help them support. An easy way, as the consumer sees immediately what a business does, the business knows the costs and there would be a bit left for our overheads. It also meant that every type of business could take part: lawyer, accountant, restaurant, printer or fish and chip shop. The concept was scalable, affordable and would have huge impact. When we started to communicate the message, the feedback was not what we hoped for –very slow actually. At first we didn't know what to do. The reason for this was that it was immediately clear what we set out to do but it took too much explaining to members as they had to figure out and decide how much they wanted to give back. It was too complicated for a business to say yes to immediately. Nowadays, what works is something we get instantly – like Twitter, a simple 1-2-3. Join here and take part. So again we went back to the drawing board.

We already knew that asking a membership fee for our basic membership was not the answer. That is another bottleneck which stops businesses from taking part. In the midst of this, I had a meeting with a guy here in London who works together with the UN. We brainstormed together; he listened and advised me that 100% of the donations had to go back to the cause. Of course he was right, but how do we manage that? We were already committed to full transparency but we have our overheads and they need to be paid. I realised he was right, so when I came out of the meeting I called my business partner Iain who lives in the Gold Coast; it was the middle of the night for him. We discussed it and didn't have an answer but we knew the guy was correct and we promised ourselves that we would only proceed if we could get it right and 100% of the donations would go to the good causes.

This got us stuck for a few months and we lost a few team members in that time who went off to do other things. While I was doing a few other projects, I gained some serious insights. Typically, as a creative person you think you can do everything and, in the process, you lose others as it becomes too complicated to communicate your message. It is a very common mistake which happens often. I learned that by doing just one thing you can be really big within your niche. By doing just one thing we could make an even bigger difference than by trying to do everything. My background is food; it is my passion, it is my purpose and I have a lot of experience in it.

In the meantime, we researched many other ideas – our own and from others – to see what we could do with them. Most importantly, we looked at what ideas work and why other ideas don't work. We thought about fundraising sites where charities had a page, toolbars which gave back for every click. Too technical for our skills and others were doing it already. I researched a very cool application called greenanysite.com. Basically, it pops up every time you want to pay for something online and if you click on Green This, the affiliate code it receives is donated to a green cause. I will definitely do something with this idea once we are established a bit more. As is often the case, why do some crazy ideas take off and others which you believe are utterly brilliant struggle and never grow or are not picked up by the public?

Just one thing. So we focus on food only, we add a charge to meals sold. Hey – it has been there all the time! This has become a very clear and concessive message: wherever you buy a meal, you pay 20 pence extra to help somebody in need. From café to top restaurant and from ready meals to take-aways, every meal would contribute to end hunger. Just one thing; when you see our logo you know exactly what it stands for: every time you eat a meal, they eat a meal. In the summer of 2009, I saw a video about the London Food Festival which simply said 'London serves more than one billion meals a year in its restaurants.' Immediately, the penny dropped and I saw the mechanism, how we could work this. You hear about inspired light bulb moments and this was definitely one of those for me.

"With money you can't buy wisdom, you can't buy inner peace. Wisdom and inner peace must be created by yourself."

Dalai Lama

What that means for restaurants is that our concept is set up in a way that all kinds of food outlets will be able to take part, with no extra fees. There is nothing else a restaurant needs to do. When joining, we supply them with leaflets to communicate with their customers why they are asked to pay 20 pence, explaining the concept. We supply texts for their website, menu, advertising or even banners. A restaurant can do more programs if they want but there is absolutely nothing they have to organise. We took away all the bottlenecks so it is totally foolproof to join. The restaurants pay us automatically every month for the number of meals they have sold, taking away all the pressure and ensuring the customer that their donations go to the good causes we work with.

In the research I did in the year I worked on the concept, I spent a lot of time looking at charities: what they do in fundraising, why it works or, more often, why it doesn't work. We spent time looking how we could improve things. I found that many charities did the same as all the other ones. Few are actually really innovative; of course, it is not their strength and they simply don't have the resources. Just asking a donor for money is not good enough any more. Donors want to know what you are going to do with their money, how it is spent and how effective you are at it. There are many reports about charities which can't produce reports about their spending or simply misinform the public. In order to grow, you have to be totally transparent.

Customers will choose food outlets which show what they do in giving back. Being part of our concept does exactly that for a member. When you choose an Extraordinary Ones member restaurant or food outlet, you know you help to feed somebody. Being part is a win-win situation. The customers pay the 20 pence extra; this way they feel they have contributed and you have a choice not to take part. Every establishment can also take part now, even in financially challenging times, as there is absolutely no risk for the business. It only adds to it and helps to get more customers coming through the door.

So how do we pay for our overheads? How do we make money when 100% of the donations go to the causes? I have set up Extraordinary Ones as a social enterprise; at the same time we have the Extraordinary Ones Foundation. All the donations go through the Foundation to the causes we work with; the trustees take care of this. Our published accounts are fully transparent. The social enterprise will take care of all the overheads being paid. We have set up a social enterprise on purpose as I strongly believe that charities have to start working as businesses. Working as a business gives you a certain mindset, attitude and energy. The sole purpose of our enterprise is to help end world hunger; we do that by coming up with innovative ways of fundraising. Keeping the donations and the business part separate doesn't just give transparency, it also allows for the fact we can't spend any of the donations at all. I have seen in some charities I have worked with that there is no sense of urgency. The effectiveness of their operations often means that less money goes to the actual good work and quite a bit is wasted on unnecessary overheads. We also will attract better quality staff in the business who will want to do good and be rewarded for it. When we are successful and feed millions, the business part will also be very successful.

This set-up gives us many opportunities. Besides raising funds, what we are basically doing is building a brand, as we share our logo and it will become more visible. The visibility will make the value of the brand bigger. This has a dual effect: not only will we be able to get more members and raise more funds, the social enterprise will also be more successful, helping to grow our innovative models.

We have set up partnerships with companies who are in the food industry. They have an interest in the same kind of companies and consumers as we do: food outlets selling meals and the customers who buy them. The win-win situation for the partners is they get exposure exactly where and when they want and are being connected to set up a good cause. We have found that everyone not only loves our concept, they also get it in an instant because of its simplicity.

Press and media are always looking for new ideas to write about and this has given us a lot of exposure already. We definitely have a new concept. Many of our members are celebrity chefs which adds to the interest of the other chefs and it adds to our partners. Our focus is on a regular stream of news items we can send out to the press rather than one big action a year, so Extraordinary Ones stays in the news.

Another interesting part of revenue we will be adding to our mix is the licensing of branded products. As our brand recognition grows, we will become more interesting for a licensing partner. We aim to sell food and related products under our name; you can think of specialised food boxes, ready meals, spices and related products. A percentage of every product will go towards hunger and the profit is used to pay our overheads and to grow the company. This is an interesting concept for both parties as our strong brand message and brand recognition will help sell the products.

"Motivation gets you through the day, but inspiration lasts a lifetime."

Nick Vujicic

The importance of a proven concept is often undervalued, especially with start-ups or innovative concepts. I knew that when I finally had the idea, it was important to prove that it works, prove that consumers will buy your product at the price you set. We organised a small press conference in Maastricht on the 15th of October 2009. We invited the local press, three TV stations, newspapers and a few restaurants. They all covered our story and the public immediately loved what we set out to do. Now we had a proven concept, people saw that the idea had developed and that things were actually happening. When you have a proven concept, there is something others can connect with.
The first thing you need now is to promote your product. When you are getting well-known enough, you need to start building your team.

Without a proven concept, many ideas never take off because others don't see the value of your idea yet. Collaboration is key to achieving your goal and you need to give others value in order to connect with you.

Immediately, I started to make connections with people who could help us grow our concept. The best opportunities always come from people who come to you, and they do so because they connect and see advantages for themselves in what you have set out to do. A few weeks after our first small event, I had a call from the tourist board who wanted to collaborate with us on a food event they had planned with 50 restaurants in early February – a beautiful opportunity to which we said yes. The tourist board organised a great week-long event, got 50 restaurants involved and organised all press and media. As a result, we had media coverage throughout the whole country for hardly any effort from our side. We had two celebrities presenting our official launch. Most importantly, the connections we have from that event are just staggering: Fifteen restaurant; Iens, the largest independent restaurant site; an advertising agency; a few sponsors; and many more opportunities.

By going slower you are actually going faster. What I mean by that is you have to make sure that you keep doing what you are best at and choose the right strategy. When you do that, connected truly to your purpose, the right partners can't help but show up and connect. The tourist board saw immediately the value for them by connecting to our causes. Every meal sold by 50 restaurants in Maastricht helped a child that week. The publicity we had was good for Extraordinary Ones and for the tourist board and restaurants. We could never have done this on our own; I knew from the beginning that knocking on individual restaurant doors is not the way forward for us. As I am writing this, we are organising a national campaign and are preparing different countries to start as well. We will get consumers to help us to get restaurants to join, making it fun and exciting. By deciding on the right strategy, proving that our concept works and acting totally in line with our purpose, the right partners are showing up for us. The speed of them showing up will get faster and faster. In this process, you have to be sure that you are totally focused on your goal and say no to anything which doesn't help you in achieving your goal. Also be careful and keep an eye out for the opportunities which present themselves to you as many of us are often so set in the way we are doing things, we don't recognise opportunities when they reach us.

When you face challenges or don't get the results you are hoping for, go back into yourself and establish why that is. In business that works exactly the same. We are now organising a national campaign in the Netherlands and when you are reading this that campaign has probably happened. What I realised myself only last week is that I have to let others who are experts take control and organise it for us. Trust them that they will do a better job than I could do, allowing the space for them to do their work. This is one of the most valuable lessons I had out of XL. When you create a playground for others to play in, then they will come and together you can create something very big. With Extraordinary Ones we have created that playground. In other words, by creating a business where we add value to each other, our collective skills and products create something more powerful. Find the right partners and trust them to do their work; especially as a creator/founder it is often difficult to let go but what you need to do is to get out of the way.

When you are following this process you can let the magic unfold, step back and enjoy.

Transformational giving is all about becoming one

Becoming more connected is really the bigger picture of Extraordinary Ones and the motivation behind our name. We are all extraordinary, and it is extraordinary if we care more for each other and give others the opportunity to be extraordinary, to have the same opportunities as we do. Ones stands for sharing what we have, we connect and become all one. The fact that we all do small (or even tiny) actions every day for the people around us wherever they are shifts us. It is so powerful that every action you do, you share that with someone else for mutual purpose. So when you buy a meal for yourself you also help feed somebody else. When you open yourself to give you also open yourself to receive. Receiving is different from taking. Taking happens from the 'self' or the ego. Taking for yourself happens when you are disconnected and believe that having ever more helps you to be happier and that you need more in your life. When you are connected to your higher purpose and you give, you always receive whatever it is you need to make your dream a reality. Open your hand, as when you give something to somebody, the signal or gesture is exactly the same as when you receive something.

Giving and receiving creates flow; if you stay connected to it, the flow will become ever stronger, like a river, and this allows you to connect to your purpose even more. Start the giving and let the magic happen.

Transformational giving

Chapter 12

What happens when we all truly connect?

Is it an idealist view to believe that we can all become truly connected again, see the end of poverty and the restoration of our planet become a reality? Well is it? We live in a time when more and more people feel there is more going on, this feeling or movement is growing ever faster. As our challenges become increasingly more pressing and time is running out, the belief that we have to find other ways is growing.

"What I hold for myself ultimately will turn rancid; what I give away and give back, obviously just creates more and more good, for myself as well as others."

Richard Gere

2012 and the new cycle of the Mayan calendar are becoming ever closer. Buckminster Fuller calls it the final exam. Everywhere you hear talk about change. There is a growing movement of people, a civil movement. Just imagine that we are correct. Just imagine what that world would look like. We all start living from the heart; truly connect with who we are and why we are here. We live a life of purpose and meaning. You have joy and pleasure in what you do, you do every day what you are best at and you use your skills to the fullest. Everything you need is there for you and we live in a world of enough. There is already enough of everything to go round for each and every one of us.

There will be enough bus drivers, enough accountants and not too many coaches, trainers or chefs. We will have clean, renewable energy and no more animals will be threatened by extinction. We will be adding net impact to the planet instead of taking from it. Reforestation will have made a big impact on our planet, we have enough water, food is grown locally and we managed to stop the rise in temperature. Nobody goes to bed hungry, everyone has the opportunity to go to school, have medical treatment and lives in a decent house.

The planet came with a set of instructions, but we seem to have misplaced them. Important rules like 'don't poison the water, soil, or air, don't let the Earth get overcrowded and don't touch the thermostat' have been broken. Buckminster Fuller said that Spaceship Earth was so ingeniously designed that no-one has a clue that we are on one. Flying through the universe at a million miles per hour, with no need for seatbelts, lots of room in the coach and really good food.

"If you have a sense of caring for others, you will manifest a kind of inner strength in spite of your own difficulties and problems."

Dalai Lama

We would be happy and manage to get along with each other. Does that sound like heaven to you? Maybe it is, but should we have to wait until we die in order to live like that? Everything in life has a balance and we have learned about that. The balance is disturbed so badly it will be difficult to make it right if we don't take quick action. In a world where we all live from our heart, of course we will still have our challenges, they will never go away. What will be different is the way you deal with them.

'Be still like a mountain and flow like a river' is an old Chinese saying. Think about it, this is so true. Nature is still and grows in silence. Mother Teresa said we need silence to touch souls. It is the silence in between notes which makes you enjoy the music. Your thoughts come from silence; in order to have silence you need inner peace and to be still. Wisdom and inner peace come from within.

Buckminster Fuller made a commitment when he was 33 years old and his child was born that he would work 50 years to make Spaceship Earth a better place. What is your commitment? What is your legacy going to be? What are you going to be remembered for?

Don't be put off by what others believe is impossible. When you state your purpose and goal, some people will tell you that it is not possible and can't be done. Listen to your inner self and guidance and you will find the right people around you to make your dreams come true.

Have a look around you; everything we need is already there. When you look around, do you see the right things? We miss so much of what is around us just because of our perception. We have taken too many things for granted. Imagine that the stars would come out only once every one hundred years. We would all stay up that night and celebrate. There is so much beauty and magic in our world which we don't even see anymore. Each of us is as complex and beautiful as all the stars in the universe.

"What the mind can conceive and believe, the mind of men can achieve."

Napoleon Hill

What is out there – the stars and the universe – are also within you. The living world is not 'out there' somewhere, but in your heart. What higher purpose are you stepping up to?

"Be yourself, because everyone else is already taken."

Oscar Wilde

Nobody to bed hungry

My higher purpose is to see the end of world hunger. Hunger is the most basic form of poverty and I believe nobody should go to bed hungry. So my commitment for the rest of my life is:

I commit to work together with others so nobody will ever have to go to bed hungry.

I have described within this book how I found my higher purpose and how my whole life has prepared me to take on this challenge. As I am writing this, Extraordinary Ones is really taking off. By the time you read this, hopefully you are contributing and so are the restaurants around you. Millions of people are working on ending world hunger and we hope to work together with many of them as we can solve it by working together. Of course, I have defined my goals and have many ideas and plans on what we can do to make it happen. Everything I do will serve my end goal and my legacy: nobody to bed hungry.

If an activity doesn't serve my purpose, it shouldn't be one of my core activities. Of course I support others around climate change, greening, nature or animals but my focus will be totally on my purpose.

"To meet the challenge of this century, human beings will have to develop a greater sense of universal responsibility."

Dalai Lama

What legacy are you going to leave?

Mary Oliver writes in her poem *Dreams*: 'One day you finally knew what you had to do, and began.'

What is it you would like to be known for?

Have I inspired you? Have you found your higher purpose? Do you know the one thing you want to commit your life to? What is it you are going to make happen? Write your idea down, share it with others. I would love to hear what your commitment is and how you are going to make it happen. Write to me at leon@feedingpeoplebook.com

Chapter 12 What happens when we all truly connect?

"For a community to be whole and healthy, it must be based on people's love and concern for each other."

Millard Fuller

About the author

From chef to social entrepreneur and visionary.
Leon Aarts's love of food has been running like a thread
through his life. He was born in the gastronomical city of
Maastricht in the Netherlands. He started his career as
a chef in some of Europe's best restaurants and later he
became the owner of a top restaurant. He was always
looking for the best ingredients and trying to innovate,
striving to be the best.

In 2001 he moved to London to start a fine food
company delivering direct to the top end restaurant trade.
The company became very successful and in 2006 Leon
became member of an international group of social
entrepreneurs which was a major turning point in his life.
He decided to find his core purpose and live his life totally
in his purpose.

Leon's vision became "Nobody to bed hungry" and the
mission is that we all become interconnected, and that is
when he founded Extraordinary Ones.

Leon's story is the story of one person's life so far, the way one theme has resurfaced in different guises during that lifetime and how he used his experiences to make a huge difference and inspire people.

"Don't ask yourself what the world needs; ask yourself what makes you come alive. And then go and do that. Because what the world needs are people who have come alive."

Howard Thurman

www.leonaarts.com
www.extraordinaryones.com

1140824R0

Printed in Great Britain by
Amazon.co.uk, Ltd.,
Marston Gate.